TopGear

SUPERCARS

THE WORLD'S FASTEST CARS

'Supercars. The purest and most extreme expression of automotive performance there is...'

TopGear

SUPERCARS

THE WORLD'S FASTEST CARS

BBC
BOOKS

pg160

pg066

pg196

pg100

CONTENTS

pg040

pg023

pg229

pg153

They're expensive, useless, inefficient, wasteful, dirty and noisy. They're ostentatious and gaudy and not particularly easy to live with. Some of them are frightening. Many are hard to drive. Most are hard to even see out of. But boy do we love them – we love them with our very souls. Supercars. The purest and most extreme expression of automotive performance there is, trundling around the roads and revving their engines and raising a single finger to automotive political correctness everywhere. Long may it continue.

Supercars will always be with us, of course, because there will always be a demand for fast, spectacular automobiles. But they're changing, because they have to change. Soon they will need to become cleaner by law. There can be no argument against the logic of that, of course, but who knows how the drive to ever-greater efficiency will shape things? Perhaps we'll look back on the early 21st century and say: 'that was the golden age'. So let's enjoy these magnificent supercars while we can. Here are the best of the best, as brought to you by Top Gear Magazine. Enjoy.

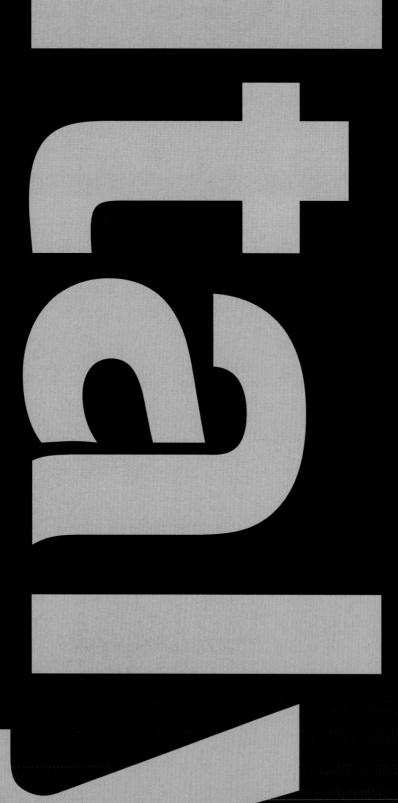

Italy isn't kicking off our book by accident. This country *is* supercars. You only need to see the spirit of the Ferrari *tifosi* at the Italian Grand Prix to understand the reverence held for the Prancing Horse.

It's a global phenomenon, too: pictures of Ferraris adorn kids' walls and tee-shirts from Paris to Peking to Perth. But dig deeper and you discover that other great names have equally glorious reputations – names like Lamborghini, Maserati and Pagani, while Alfa Romeo's is surely greatest of them all.

They even sound fast. *Belissimo!*

Open Season

The LP640 is not just the ultimate Lamborghini, it's the ultimate car, full stop. **Bill Thomas** enjoys a wild, and possibly final, ride

BADASS. IT ISN'T A TERM I'D have used to describe this car if left to my own devices, but the excited young Californian guy who stopped his motorbike to talk to us as we photographed the new Lamborghini Murciélago LP640 Roadster used the phrase as soon as he heard the engine spec. A 6.5-litre V12 revving to 8,000rpm, pumping out 631bhp and capable of pushing the car to 205mph? And it looks like this? Two metres wide? And it's yellow?

"That is a *badass* car."

Yes, it is. We needn't dwell on what badass means precisely – 'naughty bottom car' or 'antisocial derrière car' doesn't quite have the same yank jive assonance. But badass has perfect assonance. Not only is it the most badass Lamborghini of all, you could argue that Lambo makes the most badass cars of all. Ipso facto, this is the most badass car of all. Drive it for more than three seconds and you'll have no reason to think differently.

Minus a roof, the Roadster is even more evil to look at than the Murciélago LP640 coupe, and that thing's a physical shock when you see it on the road. This masterpiece is visually stimulating enough to make pedestrian onlookers' heads explode in showers of blood and brain matter – I saw it happen, I swear.

It's a mind-ripping concept car made real, then given one of the world's most fabulous engines and plenty of development time with some of the world's great chassis engineers and test drivers. It is a brutal, beautiful supercar, styled by Luc Donckerwolke, a Peruvian-born Belgian who's done the Italians proud. This is a car that does justice to the great Miura and other Italian supercars drawn on paper by proper maestros, sporting a cigarette in one hand, a pencil in the other and five or six naked, buxom women whispering sweet inspiration in both ears at

once. Long may that style continue. Long live Luc Donckerwolke. We like your work, sir.

Let's enjoy this monster while cars like this are allowed to exist. Its shock-and-awe visual power comes from its ungodly lowness and extreme width, combined with its incredible proportions in profile, with that cab-forward stance and a long, long tail. It doesn't need a giant rear wing, nor any aerodynamic addenda – the large scoops in the flanks pop out at speed to help cool the engine. Look at the exhaust pipe: you'd need to double-check you knew where the dog was before starting up. Viewed from dead rear, the tail strakes blend inward toward the cabin and flank the bonnet in a twisting, crazy warp of vents and lines. The engine cover is still too high to let you see much out of the central rearview mirror, but it doesn't matter – looking behind is one of the least important things you'll do in the Lamborghini Murcielago LP640 Roadster.

A roof is packed into the small boot beneath the nose, but frankly it's an apology, a difficult-to-fit canvas contraption that is an emergency get-you-home. It can only be used at speeds below 100mph, so it's particularly useless in the LP640 Roadster, which is cabable of more than double that.

We surely don't need that roof contraption today. It's a perfect, crisp Los Angeles December morning and one of America's great roads beckons – Highway 74, the Ortega Highway, which winds across the hills between Lake Elsinore and San Juan Capistrano.

It's an event, this car – an occasion on four 18-inch wheels. It starts with the styling, of course, as you walk up to the car, then you dip a handle beside the glass and raise the scissor door straight up. Magnificent. Sliding in is easy, and you find yourself sitting in a body-hugging bucket seat that's not quite as comfortable as it should be,

and a driving position that's not quite as natural as it should be. You sit miles away from the dash and even more miles behind the incredible sloping windscreen, behind a wheel that telescopes out a long, long way. It's almost – but not quite – far enough to prevent a classic long-arm, short-leg Italian driving position. My legs were way too splayed with the wheel up close where I needed it, but I didn't care and neither would you. Obviously the car feels wide and low and strange, but you soon get used to it – as soon as you move away, you feel that the big Lambo's on your side. It is not daunting.

The new dials are attractive and easy to use and far more appealing than the stuck-in Kenwood Afterthought Model nav/stereo system, which is a crime on a car of this price – about £200,000 – but somehow appealing too. There are traces of Italian-ness here that the German masters of Lamborghini seem to understand. Does it really matter that the cabin still feels a bit thrown together, despite the improvement in fit and finish instigated by Audi? No. Nothing matters, not the stereo, not the build quality, nothing. Just fire up the engine, get driving and start forgetting every reference you ever had with normal cars. Here we go – time to explore this thing's utterly explosive performance.

And here the Murciélago LP640 Roadster reveals its greatest trick – the driving experience lives up to and then surpasses the expectation you build up from the car's appearance. Walking around it, looking at it and sitting in it just doesn't in any way prepare you for how fabulous it is to drive; to accelerate, brake, corner and – perhaps most unforgettably of all – to listen to.

The V12's starter turns over gruffly for three seconds before the recalcitrant big lump cranks

The doors that have adorned every boy's wall since the 1980s

Engine- cooling vents open when the Roadster is really cooking

n 34 secs.
wing roof does
g to reduce speed

'Let's clack the badass throttle pedal all the way to the badass cabin floor as soon as she's warm. Now we're moving'

Dash looks like an air traffic controller's worst nightmare

into life. At tickover it sounds like the sort of unit any decent tractor manufacturer (like Lamborghini) would produce – like a tractor. There is a mechanical threshing noise from the top end, a bit like that made by your grandma's sewing machine – it's pure machinery, with no aural excellence whatever. Nowhere near as sonorous as a V6 Golf, for instance, and something tweaks your brain to think that you might start to become disappointed. But it doesn't matter. Tickover means nothing to an engine like this. It doesn't want to tick over.

Blip the throttle and it sounds beefier, more tonal and... badass, and the chassis twitches in response. But not much – it is immensely tortionally strong, this chopped car, helped by extra carbon-fibre crossbracing in the engine bay. Only the very harshest potholes induce any shake in the steering column and dash. Lambo has got this bit dead right, and the claimed weights for coupe and Roadster are the same. It is quite heavy, tipping the scales at 1,665kg. It's four-wheel drive too, remember, its electronic Viscous Traction system delivering up to 100 per cent of torque to the front or rear axles, depending on conditions – in normal driving, 70 per cent of drive is delivered to the rear wheels.

We're aboard the clutch pedal-less manual E-gear model here, which is slightly disappointing – I'd always choose a manual over even the best of these paddle-shift systems. Changing gear is an event when you have an open gate, and your brain imprints the motion of each change, so you remember where you are in the 'box. Not here – one flick is the same as another, so it would take a while to get to know the car and

the engine revs at various speeds. Not to worry, flick the right-hand paddle toward you – right is up, left is down – and the automatic clutch engages smoothly, moving the big car away.

Let's clack the badass throttle pedal all the way to the badass cabin floor as soon as she's warm. Now we're moving. I drove the previous Murciélago – and the Diablo and Countach before that – and this thing is much, much faster. Not sure whether it clicked with you how new and wonderful this Murciélago in LP640 form is, but take it from me, it is properly rapid, a mind-shattering car.

The engine revs smoothly and quickly. There's plenty of torque down low, then as the needle rips up the rev range, things start to get hairy – the howl gets deeper, the thrust harder and suddenly the 'box has changed up for you at about 8,000rpm – 62mph arrives in 3.4secs, 0.4secs quicker than its predecessor. *Badass.*

Cornering is epic. The balance is largely neutral and you never get the impression the car is particularly heavy. It changes direction with great confidence, and the steering transmits an amazing amount of feel, especially when you get to the point when the tyres start to make a soft 'swish' sound and you approach the limit of adhesion.

That's when you need the steering to communicate with you and it does, lightening up just enough to let you know you're about to run short of grip. Grab another gear in this state and the nose jerks inward quite violently as the throttle comes off, but not enough to unsettle the tail – there's too much grip for that.

Probably the best way to slide this car on dry tarmac would be to trail-brake into a corner –

the brakes seem to have enough rear bias to encourage that sort of behaviour, but you'd be going so fast at entry that you'd need a track to prove it. Or at least, I would. Speeds are very high when you get to the limit of these tyres (13 inches wide at the rear).

The cockpit remains relatively quiet and free of buffeting, no matter what speed you're doing, but taller drivers will get a slightly uncomfortable blast of air to the very top of their heads – that air was hitting my noggin at pretty high speeds on the way back to Santa Ana, but at no point was I anything other than comfortable.

At one stage, as the road opened out into a long downhill straight dotted with very little traffic, even the idiot that is yours truly thought twice about trying for 205mph. But the car was still accelerating hard at unmentionable speed, and with no roof and the glorious wail of the big V12 bouncing off the Armco, 205mph seemed superflous. You only need 60mph.

No supercar gets close to this thing, and possibly never will. Maybe we've reached a zenith here – maybe the Germans will put too much German-ness into the Murciélago's replacement. I won't (and you probably won't) ever have the sort of wealth to be able to throw away £200,000 on a car. But anyone who is that lucky should put the LP640 on their list.

It makes the Gallardo Spyder seem about as hard as a Kia Picanto 1.0S. Yes, Jeremy, it really is that badass.

Schuey

Story by Bill Thomas Photography by John Wycherley

Even in retirement Michael Schumacher was still helping Ferrari stay on top. The Italians' awesome new supercar, the F430 Scuderia, is the direct result of the German's obsessive attention to detail

woz 'ere

S CUD. WALK UP TO IT. LOW, sleek, more purposeful, more evil than other modern Ferraris. It's going to take you somewhere and it's going to do it in its own way. Point to note: the stripes are painted, they are not decals. Lots of aggressive aero stuff going on too, much more than on the F430, which is hardly a placid looking car in standard form. But the Scuderia is not really an F430. It is not what the Challenge Stradale was to the F360. It's a new machine. These are aero sculptings: not aesthetic but functional, honed in a wind-tunnel, the lips and curves and intakes in the front air dam, the complexities of the underbody, the workings of the massive rear diffuser with higher-mounted exhaust outlets all designed to help improve airflow and downforce. Not that the aesthetics are bad – on our red machine, the graphite wheels match the silver-grey stripes beautifully. It is not overdone, it is not underdone. It is 15mm lower than an F430 and that's perfectly lower.

Scud. Open the driver's door. Handle works easily, with a positive, meaty click. Door isn't heavy, swings out wide. Carbon-fibre door trims inside. These look great – and so do the lightweight carbon-fibre racing seats trimmed in alcantara. Magnificent seats. Point to note:

no carpets. Just bare metal flooring and exposed welding on the chassis. No need for carpet, and all of the sound deadening stuff has been stripped out too. Your eye works around the metal floor. Alloy pedals. Simple trim. Racer.

Scud. Slide your legs in under the superb leather-trimmed wheel and drop down into the body-hugging bucket. The wheel's set a bit low. An Italian test driver has been in this car. Find the column release. There it is, down to the left of the column. Up. It comes up far enough, telescopes toward you. Get the seat back a tad. Legs aren't too bent. Wheel clears them. Good driving position. Nearly Porsche-good, but not quite. Look forward and you see a red bulge of bodywork over the front left wheel arch, dropping out of sight as it flows down toward the centre of the bonnet. Proper low sports car, convex screen, mirrors long and slender outside, large and useful inside. Adjust. There is a large perspex window immediately behind your head, wide and expansive, with the 510bhp V8 behind it, all cam covers and carbon-fibre airboxes, and beyond that, the large rear screen, in weight-saving Lexan. A supercar you can see out of. Bonus.

Scud. Hunker down in the seat, look around. Big, useful, ball air vents. No radio. No cruise or nav or extra flim-flam. Carbon fibre all over the

shop. Big alien-stun-tazer carbon-fibre gear shift blades behind the wheel. To call these finely-sculpted works of art 'paddles' is obscene. Paddles are what you use to make canoes or river steamers go through water, or to play ping-pong with. These are blades. Used for scything up and down gears. Reach back behind your left shoulder, beyond the wide bolsters of the seats, back there somewhere, seatbelt buckle, draw it round, down, click.

Scud. Deep breath. Turn the key, turn it right round to the stop. Every light on the dash makes itself known but the engine doesn't fire. Ah, the starter button, on the steering wheel. My God, what a beautiful steering wheel, what a beautiful alloy manettino switch, and what a beautiful red starter button. Punch it? No, not just yet, let's think about this car first, think about what it is.

It ain't no Fiat Stilo Schumacher special edition. Remember that litter? Schuey agreed to put his name to it and I almost vomited when I heard about it. It was even worse than the Seicento Sporting Schumacher a few years before. At least that thing had character. Of course, Michael had nothing to do with either car, just marketing spin.

But now, right now, we're sitting in a car that the seven-time world F1 champion *did* have ⋮

V8 engine revs beyond 8,500 – and the yellow dial to measure it is uber-cool

This little Scuderia badge – and the rest of the car – will cost you a cool £175,000

430 SCUDERIA

'Right now, we're sitting in a car that the seven-time world champion had a lot to do with. It doesn't bear his name, but he's been at work here. Schuey's Scud'

RACE

SPORT

a lot to do with. It doesn't bear his name, but he's been hard at work here. Schuey has made this car what it is. Schuey's Scud.

"We had to put an unmarked full-face helmet on him when he tested it at the Nordschleife," says Michele Giaramita, Scud tech boss. "Just so people didn't see it was him." His lap time around there? Ferrari isn't saying, but the knowing smiles of the engineers tell a story of their own.

"Michael made a lot of time for us with this car," continues Michele, "because he has retired from F1, of course. He enjoyed helping us, enjoyed it more than going to F1 races as a consultant, maybe, and yes, the Nürburgring was part of it. But Fiorano (Ferrari's test track at Maranello) is this car's benchmark, not the Nordschleife – and around Fiorano, the Scuderia's lap time and the Enzo's are the same."

Scud. The tech highlights are as follows: a 100kg weight saving over the F430, down to a 1,350kg kerb weight. Hollow front and rear anti-roll bars, titanium springs and wheel nuts, lighter shocks and steering box, lighter front and rear bumpers, and undertray and diffuser contribute to the saving. Then a comprehensive strip job and carbon-fibre-isation inside, some lighter components in the engine bay, plus that Lexan rear screen to finish it off. Brake discs are carbon ceramic, 18mm larger in diameter than the F430's, with six-pot calipers front and rear.

Power for the 4.3-litre, 90degree V8 is up to 510bhp at 8,500rpm, mostly as a result of intake and exhaust tuning. Ferrari is also proud of its new ECU, which is capable of monitoring the ionising currents generated inside the combustion chamber between the spark-plug electrodes. What that means in English is more efficient, faster sparking, F1-style. Compression ratio is up to 11.88:1. And all this is delivered to the road through a superb new automated manual gearbox called F1-SuperFast 2, which reduces shift times, in Race mode, to only 60 milliseconds (599 is 100ms, F430 is 150ms), which makes it the fastest of any gearbox of its kind anywhere. The Scud runs to 62mph in under 3.6secs, to 124mph in less than 11.6secs and blasts through a standing klick in 20.9 seconds, which is about the same as a 599 and only a second or so slower than an Enzo. Top speed is 198mph.

Scud. Punch the starter button. Short whirr, then a breezy, cammy zim as the engine fires. Blip the throttle and it's all no-resistance, no-flywheel lightness, very precise throttle response, hard, flat exhaust note, nothing Yank-V8 about it, a shrill, tingling whap-thrap, a bark, not a rumble. ∴

'Punch the starter button. Short whirr, then a breezy, cammy zing as the engine fires. Blip the throttle, and there's a shrill, tingling whap-thrap'

F430 Scud –
almost as fast
as an Enzo and
faster than a 599

'Nail the Scud throttle pedal right to the metal floor.
Christ, this thing moves, it leaps forward with brutal
intensity. A glorious wail emits from the engine'

Big central rev counter needle moves swiftly, redline somewhere after 8,500, 'Sport' showing on the manettino readout screen.

Nail the Scud throttle pedal right the way to the metal floor. Christ, this thing moves – it leaps forward with brutal intensity. One-two-three-four rev warning lights Christmas-tree across the top of the steering wheel in rapid succession, whack, change up, whack, and again, whack. A glorious, hard-edged wail from the engine, high-pitched from the inside, a flat bark from the outside, relentless thrust. Steering is quite heavy but alive with info, precise and quick and in no way dead. Brakes are strong, mightily strong, and full of feel too. What a car.

Think of the raw knowledge Michael Schumacher has accumulated over the years about electronic differentials and traction control. More than me – I know what a differential does, but not precisely how it does it, nor how different settings can feel. But I'm happy to let Big Mick do the honing for me. And here, in the Scud's electronically-controlled F1-style differential, we have perhaps the most sublime of the car's technical highlights. You work the E-Diff through the manettino, which has five modes: Snow, Sport, Race, Traction Control Off and The Lot Off. Snow helps in slippery conditions. Sport is

fine for normal driving. Race gives the full-on super-bang 60ms changes and hardens the suspension. Then the two further modes allow you to spin the wheels with the safety net of stability control, or have no safety net whatsoever. And in any of these higher modes, you have the option of softening or hardening the suspension with a separate switch on the centre console.

I enjoyed driving it in Race mode, with the suspension set to soft, and the traction control turned off. That left the stability control on, you see, so you could introduce quite a radical-feeling amount of drift before the system cut in. You could drive it like an idiot, enjoy correcting the swing of oversteer (which is predictable and easy for a mid-engined car) knowing that the thing wouldn't let you get so far out of shape you'd spin and hit something.

It's magnificent in standard Race mode, too, where it leaves you slightly less yaw than with the TC off, but still gives enough to play with – enough to allow you a little bit of slide, just to give you a proper idea that the tyres are working at their best, combined with the hardness of the Race suspension, which is still compliant enough for road use. Drive to the limit of this Race traction control setting and you are driving to the limit. Or you can lean on the TC, and get

max thrust out of corners just by nailing the throttle, the engine working with the E-Diff to smoothly deliver the right amount of power to get you out of the corner – it is 40 percent more accelerative out of corners than an F430. Magic.

Ah, wonderful Scud. As I ripped around Ferrari's mountain test roads near Modena, old women wagging their fingers at me for being such an anti-social fool, other road users grinning and appreciating the immense soundtrack, I realised that I hadn't had as much fun in a car since my first drive in a Lotus Elise, 11 years ago. It is a very driveable supercar, not a daunting one like a Lambo Murciélago, yet extremely, intoxicatingly fast. The technical excellence of the electronic differential and the incredible gearbox (which is just as impressive in its lovely, progressive clutch feel during slow manoeuvring as it is with its full-power shifting) just add to the experience.

There are sports cars, and then there are Ferraris. And this latest Ferrari road car is the greatest. Probably the single greatest Ferrari ever for sheer ability and raw excitement. It is also, without a question in my buzzing head, the greatest car on the face of this earth. When someone asks me: "What's the best car you've ever driven?", my answer is a new, simple, short one.

Scud. [TG]

Experience shift paddles built like blades, wielded by an automotive Conan

LAP OF THE GODS

Dario Benuzzi, Ferrari's chief test driver, isn't just cool, he's sub-zero. When he walks into the pit garage that sits halfway down Fiorano's main straight, the temperature drops a few degrees. The technicians fussing around the FXX stiffen slightly when they see him. Other Ferrari people greet him warmly but with a certain formality. One of them refers to him as 'The Prince'

Story by Jason Barlow Photography by Barry Hayden

Vents, grilles –
the monstrous
FXX needs a whole
lot of cooling

Rear wing helps with
downforce, but the
FXX also has actuators

'This man has shown Gilles Villeneuve and Michael Schumacher where to turn and where to apply the brakes. Ferrari folklore says he was quick enough to have competed'

I FIRST MET DARIO 10 YEARS AGO. If anything, he looks even younger now than he did then. He's 63 or 64 – nobody knows for sure – and he's been test-driving Ferraris for a living since 1971. Imagine. All those BB512s, F40s, and Enzos. He has done more laps of Fiorano than any other driver, a good deal of them faster than anyone else too. This man has shown Gilles Villeneuve and Michael Schumacher where to turn left, right and apply the brakes. For a while he tested the Scuderia's F1 cars; according to Ferrari folklore he was more than quick enough to have competed at the highest level. Yet he chose never to race. Just didn't fancy the idea.

But the real key to Dario's super-cool status is that he has simply never bothered to learn English. Not a single word. Not even 'hello'. So he could be speaking Italian with the equivalent of a Brummie accent, raving about his favourite salami or rubbishing Romano Prodi, and you'd be none the wiser. He sounds fast even when he's talking slowly. Nigel Mansell always sounds slow even when he's speaking quickly.

"Buongiorno," he says to me, removing his sunglasses. Not a lock of hair is out of place. The shoes are immaculate. The eyes twinkle.

My eyes would be twinkling too, if I had an FXX to play with. This is Ferrari's skunkworks car. Ferrari people tend to refer to it as a 'mobile laboratory'; if you remember, the company invited 29 of its 'favoured' customers to participate in the experiments. Together with the Corse Clienti programme, in which Ferrari sells, runs and maintains ex-F1 cars, this is how the seriously rich get their Ferrari kicks.

I'm still dreaming about buying a used F355. Well, this is a few notches above that.

To recap: the FXX programme kicked off in late 2005. For £1m, you get the car but you also get six specially organised track events per year over the two-year period the programme is due to run. You can keep the car in your own collection or you can store it at Ferrari's HQ. In addition to the official events, Ferrari will fly the FXX and your own team of dedicated mechanics to whichever circuit you prefer.

To deter speculators all FXX owners have signed watertight contracts. Enzos – the original 399 now sadly depleted by 65 – are changing hands these days for about £750,000 so it's understandable. But there's an added element of confidentiality too. The FXX is a rolling test-bed for new Ferrari technology, an ever-evolving prototype of the next generation supercar, in which a small group of potential customers have a personal stake. Even if you're as rich as Croesus, this is as close as you can get to becoming part of the family. In exchange for your £1m you don't just get to meet and hang out with Dario; you get to be him. Do you learn to drive like him? Impossible. Besides, Dario is insistent that this isn't really the point of the programme.

"Yes, the FXX is a kind of racing car," he says, eyes increasingly a-twinkle as the words tumble mellifluously out (the presence of Ferrari's pretty Roman PR Beatrice is helping us both enormously here), "but it also has to be accessible for our customers. Of course, it is an extremely high performance car and it has to be driven. Really driven. But our customers need to feel that they can manage it, that it is not too intimidating for them.

"The best thing about the FXX? Performance, performance and performance. Though the gearbox and the brakes are very impressive too. ❯

'The FXX isn't just state-of-the-art, it's where art hopes to be in a few years' time. Even some of its bodywork scoops have scoops of their own'

[Waves arms theatrically.] All of it!" He pauses to gather his thoughts. Nothing about salami as yet.

"Look, this is a car you can take control of. It is well-balanced at the limit. The FXX programme is not about having and developing a squad of super talented drivers. What would be the point? We have Michael..."

Indeed. And Michael has an FXX. Car 30, a black one. Nobody objected to the elite 29 growing by one on account of the gatecrasher's provenance. A good performance yardstick too: apparently, at last year's FXX Nürburgring event the fastest customer was still 11 seconds adrift of Schumacher's best time. He has a great future behind him that boy.

At Fiorano, the hierarchy goes like this. This year's F1 car laps it in 58 seconds. The Enzo needs 1min 25 seconds. The less powerful F430 is only two seconds per lap slower, underlining

its remarkable pace. And the FXX? Dario's record is 1min 18, six whole seconds faster than the car that spawned it. Even with me strapped uncomfortably into the passenger seat, that's what we're aiming for today. Oh Lord.

Let's have a closer look at this thing. Up the road in the impressive new Galleria museum, you'll find all manner of gob-smackingly beautiful Ferraris. The FXX isn't beautiful, but it is certainly gob-smacking. Many of those classic Ferraris are as aerodynamically effective as a terracotta pot, whereas the FXX isn't just state-of-the-art, it's where the art hopes to be in a few years' time. Even some of its bodywork scoops have scoops of their own.

Max Mosley, the FIA's president, is always guffing on about the need for a far greater technology exchange between F1 and future road cars. The FXX provides that sort of conduit.

It features a new aero concept which combines bodywork ducts covered by flaps hooked up to a series of electro-mechanical actuators, designed to redirect air around and through the car depending on how fast it's going.

At low speeds, the air cools the FXX's internals. Above 150mph, the actuators manipulate it into generating massive downforce. Clever. Of course, a big wing would do the same job, but it would also cause drag. This way you get the downforce without the drag, although the FXX does still feature a multi-adjustable rear wing, the prominence of which depends on which circuit you're at. The upshot is 40 per cent more downforce than the Enzo delivers.

More power too. When I first sampled the FXX at Mugello in late 2005, its Enzo-sourced 6.2-litre V12 produced 789bhp somewhere north of 8,500rpm. Now it's in excess of

850bhp, proof that the car really is evolving. Other developments include a new combustion chamber and crankcase, and a new exhaust system. The gearbox boasts a shift time of less than 100 milliseconds – Felipe's F1 car can't swap cogs much quicker than that. Brembo has supplied bespoke ceramic brakes (398 x 36mm at the front, 380 x 34 at the rear); Bridgestone has used the project to hone a completely new slick tyre which is much less temperature sensitive than usual. Clearly, none of these people is messing about here.

Since the start of the programme in September 2005, the various FXXs have completed a total of 13,359 miles. We're about to add another eight.

It's a hell of a tight fit, this car. Believe me, none of the lucky 29 is a regular down the pie shop. The seats are uncomfortable even by race car standards. But that won't matter where we're

going. Dario, obviously, slots himself in with no trouble at all. Sixty-odd years of fettuccini and still no hint of middle-age spread.

The FXX's cabin is bare bones basic. Carbon fibre might be super strong but it feels strangely brittle. There's a Magneti Marelli data acquisition display for the driver and carbon fibre gearshift paddles, but the column stalks are no better than a Fiat Panda's. The master's feet will operate a throttle and brake pedal that are the same size. (Good to know that braking is taken as seriously as accelerating.) The Enzo's aircon pod now contains a start button, the ignition cut-off switch, and an anodised knob that controls the car's aero settings. There's stuff for the nervous passenger to fiddle with, but what if something falls off or ignites? Best not to touch anything.

Dario is wearing his FXX race suit and gloves; yes, your million quid also buys you some

bespoke overalls, though the logo that adorns them is rubbish. As is the name, if we're honest.

The engine is very, very far from rubbish. Even at tick-over, the sound of a V12 is one of the world's wonders. There are 48 valves behind my head but everything is well behaved. There might be Formula One blood pumping through its veins but it's cultured.

We do a warm-up lap. Let me tell you, it's not just the car that needs to get acclimatised. Dario gives it some out of the garage and that cultured engine note instantly turns primal. The valves aren't so calm now. Immediate impression: 850bhp in a car weighing 1,155kg equals bullet-from-a-gun forward motion. And he hasn't even started trying yet. Time to lodge the track's contours and corners in your memory. Fiorano, constructed in 1972 on Enzo Ferrari's instruction, is a tricky track. The section over the bridge feels ∵

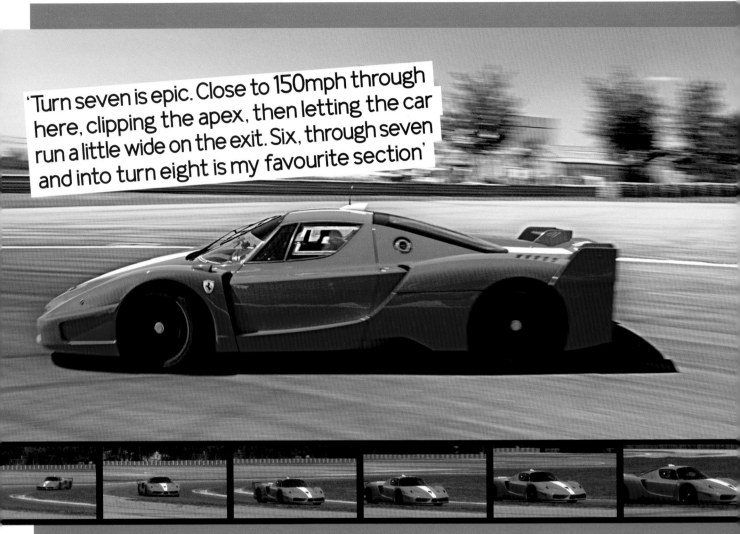

like it should go on much longer than it does. Instead, it turns right rather abruptly. The kink left towards the bottom of the main straight is scary too. God, these seats are firm.

Into the garage. Engine off. The FXX's people plug in lap-tops and insert power cables. Canadian film director David Cronenberg loves motor racing and adores Ferrari. Some of his films – the nasty ones like *Videodrome* or *The Fly* – anthropomorphise disease and machines. He'd like this: the FXX's veins are pulsing.

Off we go again. After the foreplay, the main event. Sideways onto the circuit, engine howling, slick fat back tyres scrabbling for grip, into second gear. Yep, this is fast. Into third. Holy shit. This is like being strapped to an explosion. Down into second again. Through turn one,

a long right hander. There's complete calm at the wheel, just a single smooth, linear steering input. Into third as we exit turn one and sweep into two: 95mph. You can barely feel the car loading up. There's no roll whatsoever, but I wish my internal organs were as well suspended. This is full-on.

Into three figures as we blast through turn three, then it's hard on the brakes for four, left hand flicking the paddle down into second gear: 50mph. (Three into four is Dario's favourite section of the circuit.) The briefest of respites through this right-hander. The level of available grip is head-spinning.

Up an incline and over the bridge. You know that what comes next arrives out of nowhere. But before that the FXX spins its back wheels unexpectedly over a slight crest. Dario flicks the wheel left, snuffing out the slide before it even happens. The acceleration here is insane. Then we're on the brakes again; the retardation is massive. All that speed simply evaporates. If you weren't wearing a full race harness you'd have no chance. Still no visible sense of effort from the driver, though we're clearly moving. Turn five: lots of fun that one. Drifting into the arena of the unwell now.

About 120mph down the hill and into second gear for turn six, a tight hairpin. Oversteer on

the exit, expertly gathered up. I give Dario the thumbs-up and the lines around his eyes beneath his visor illuminate his smile. How many thousands of times has he done this? Still, beats working and all that.

Turn seven is epic. Close to 150mph through here, clipping the apex, then letting the car run a little wide on the exit. Six, through seven and into turn eight: that's my favourite section. Second gear, just 40mph through here. Just enough time to catch your breath.

Then it's down the main straight past the pit garage. I've been watching people doing this all morning, and I've done it myself. Common sense dictates that you lift just before the left hand kink, or maybe brake a little. But Ferrari's drivers know not to, and watching them carry big speed through it is one of the day's highlights.

Dario probably hasn't backed off here since April 1971 and he's not about to now. Just shy of 170mph appears on the display before he buries that brake pedal into the floor. Lap over; one minute 18 seconds.

Ferrari's new supercar is due to launch in 2010. It will go, stop, steer and handle like the FXX, while using new technologies like regenerative braking and energy re-capture. Prepare to be utterly amazed.

Dario Benuzzi currently has no plans to retire.

Two-up, the FXX still laps Fiorano in one minute, eighteen seconds

Fast does not even begin to cover the speed Dario achieves

Great, another turn. Jason's internal organs struggle to realign themselves

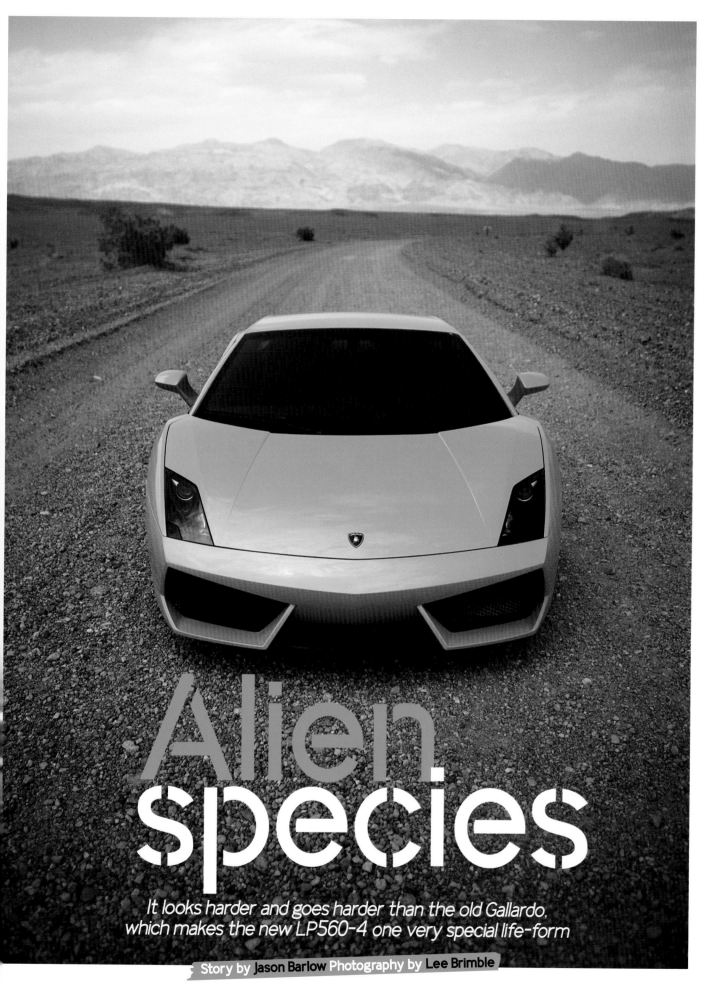

Alien species

It looks harder and goes harder than the old Gallardo,
which makes the new LP560-4 one very special life-form

Story by Jason Barlow Photography by Lee Brimble

THE 'MOVIE' VEGAS – *SWINGERS, OCEAN'S 11*, ALL the Rat Pack stuff – is a sexy, seductive, shimmering neon paradise, where lissom blondes whisper sweet nothings to Clooney or Sinatra, and dice tumble across green baize.

The 'real' Vegas is a series of gaudy hangars, where natural light is banned and the morbidly obese – willing participants in a mass lobotomy – waddle between rows of one-armed bandits. Drink yourself insensible, and it's theoretically possible to enjoy Vegas for what it is. But if ever there was a city that's all mouth and no trousers, it's this one.

Lamborghini used to be guilty of a similar 'mouth/trousers' malfunction. Few of Lambo's many owners during its 45-year existence have ever had much cash to invest in the company, so there hasn't always been the substance to back up the bravado. Granted, no one with petrol in their veins could argue with the Miura or Countach or even the Diablo. But then few with normally sized limbs could fit into them, either.

Anyway, it's the present day, and here we are inside a large inflatable marquee moored in a hotel car park in Vegas on the occasion of the launch of the new Gallardo LP560-4. The times have a-changed. Lamborghini has prospered royally under Audi ownership, and now trades under the brand banner, 'Always Different'. Tonight's dinner certainly is, not least because there's a catwalk in the middle of the table and between courses we're being treated to a 'turn'.

First some girls appear and start shimmying to the White Stripes' *Seven Nation Army*. Then a slinky blonde soprano in a white dress wanders out and begins warbling. Best of all, though, are a pair of Ninja parkour types, who leap around brilliantly, imperilling the bread rolls. Lamborghini's executives, including the impressively leonine Stephan Winkelmann, are clearly making a point here: this is no ordinary car company.

Rounding things off is a beautifully shot black-and-white film, during which a Gallardo power-slides expertly out of an LA junction and the words 'anti-boredom assist' appear on the screen. What *could* they mean?

Luckily, Lambo's financial results back up this machismo. Last year, the company sold 2,406 cars, and made a £37m pre-tax profit off sales of £369m. That's a 160 per cent increase, year-on-year. In these troubled economic times, it's more proof that the world's highest-net-worth individuals have reached a point where they're immune to the turbulence that's affecting the rest of us. Winkelmann says that the company must make the world's most desirable cars and, rather intriguingly, "be the best place to work". Brand director Manfred Fitzgerald adds that Lambos are "extreme, uncompromising and Italian", because, as he told me earlier this year, they're the "only bad boys left out there".

With Russia and Asia-Pacific now coming on-stream in a big way, there's clearly a market for this sort of bad-boy brash. The Gallardo, meanwhile, is Lamborghini's most successful ever model. More than 7,000 have been sold since 2003, and the last time I drove one, I have to say I didn't think there was much wrong with it. Which makes this the perfect time to unveil the v2.0 reboot.

Chief among the changes is the 'all-new' 5.2-litre V10 engine. It uses direct injection – *iniezione diretta stratificata*, if you want to impress your friends or alienate your girlfriend – but can still rev to 8,000rpm. Combustion is more efficient, and it's also 34bhp more powerful. But the big story here isn't what's increased, it's what's got smaller. CO_2 emissions have been reduced by 18 per cent, down to 327g/km for the 'e-gear' model. Fuel consumption has been reduced similarly (the claimed combined average is 21mpg). ⁛

New rear end deals nicely with previous-gen's stuntedness

Colour screen, knurled knobs, but same old Audi buttons. Tsk tsk

Yes, the red line *is* at 8,500rpm. We checked to make sure

18:54
12.05.2008

'We want to introduce Lamborghini's new bac

It's not the
peyote kicking
in, it really is
that colour

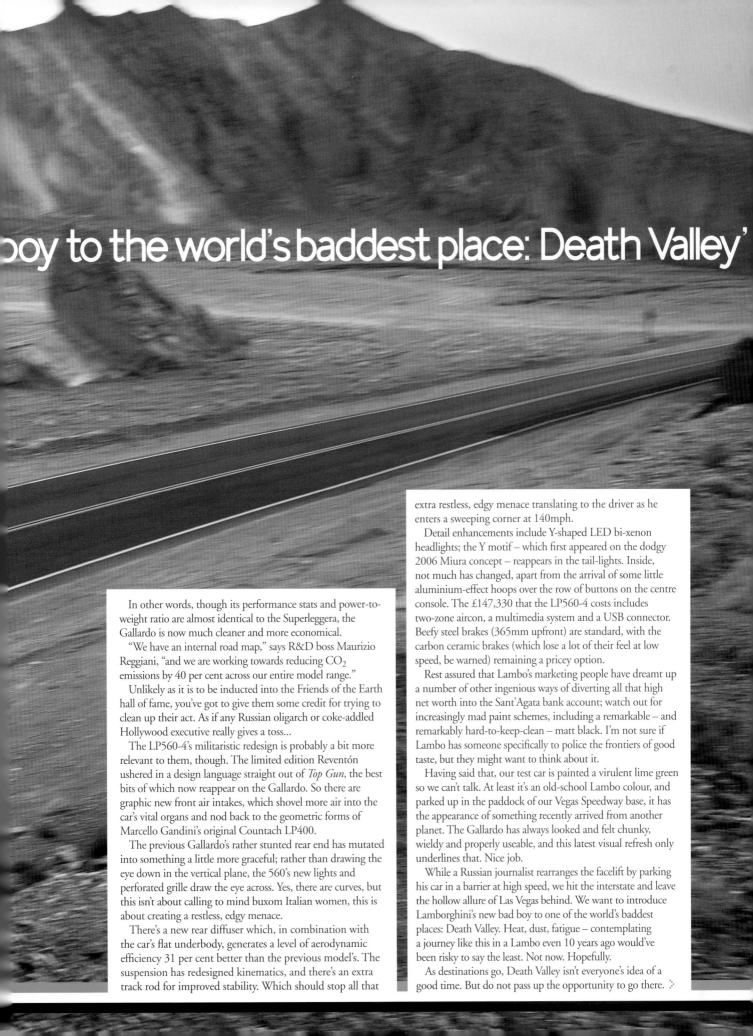

In other words, though its performance stats and power-to-weight ratio are almost identical to the Superleggera, the Gallardo is now much cleaner and more economical.

"We have an internal road map," says R&D boss Maurizio Reggiani, "and we are working towards reducing CO_2 emissions by 40 per cent across our entire model range."

Unlikely as it is to be inducted into the Friends of the Earth hall of fame, you've got to give them some credit for trying to clean up their act. As if any Russian oligarch or coke-addled Hollywood executive really gives a toss...

The LP560-4's militaristic redesign is probably a bit more relevant to them, though. The limited edition Reventón ushered in a design language straight out of *Top Gun*, the best bits of which now reappear on the Gallardo. So there are graphic new front air intakes, which shovel more air into the car's vital organs and nod back to the geometric forms of Marcello Gandini's original Countach LP400.

The previous Gallardo's rather stunted rear end has mutated into something a little more graceful; rather than drawing the eye down in the vertical plane, the 560's new lights and perforated grille draw the eye across. Yes, there are curves, but this isn't about calling to mind buxom Italian women, this is about creating a restless, edgy menace.

There's a new rear diffuser which, in combination with the car's flat underbody, generates a level of aerodynamic efficiency 31 per cent better than the previous model's. The suspension has redesigned kinematics, and there's an extra track rod for improved stability. Which should stop all that

extra restless, edgy menace translating to the driver as he enters a sweeping corner at 140mph.

Detail enhancements include Y-shaped LED bi-xenon headlights; the Y motif – which first appeared on the dodgy 2006 Miura concept – reappears in the tail-lights. Inside, not much has changed, apart from the arrival of some little aluminium-effect hoops over the row of buttons on the centre console. The £147,330 that the LP560-4 costs includes two-zone aircon, a multimedia system and a USB connector. Beefy steel brakes (365mm upfront) are standard, with the carbon ceramic brakes (which lose a lot of their feel at low speed, be warned) remaining a pricey option.

Rest assured that Lambo's marketing people have dreamt up a number of other ingenious ways of diverting all that high net worth into the Sant'Agata bank account; watch out for increasingly mad paint schemes, including a remarkable – and remarkably hard-to-keep-clean – matt black. I'm not sure if Lambo has someone specifically to police the frontiers of good taste, but they might want to think about it.

Having said that, our test car is painted a virulent lime green so we can't talk. At least it's an old-school Lambo colour, and parked up in the paddock of our Vegas Speedway base, it has the appearance of something recently arrived from another planet. The Gallardo has always looked and felt chunky, wieldy and properly useable, and this latest visual refresh only underlines that. Nice job.

While a Russian journalist rearranges the facelift by parking his car in a barrier at high speed, we hit the interstate and leave the hollow allure of Las Vegas behind. We want to introduce Lamborghini's new bad boy to one of the world's baddest places: Death Valley. Heat, dust, fatigue – contemplating a journey like this in a Lambo even 10 years ago would've been risky to say the least. Not now. Hopefully.

As destinations go, Death Valley isn't everyone's idea of a good time. But do not pass up the opportunity to go there. ⁙

'With four-wheel drive, and shod in new low-rolling-resistance Pirelli P Zeroes, the Gallardo is blessed with other-worldly levels of grip'

Quilted seats for comfort and the ultimate in absorbency

Owners from Las Vegas have option of 'kerb crawl' button

Head south out of Vegas on the I-15, then west on the Blue Diamond Road, towards Pahrump. You can't miss it. You can't miss it because, once you've cleared the gas stations, single-storey shops and soulless malls that stud the edge of every major American city, there is *nothing to miss*.

And I mean nothing. You crest the top of a rise, modest mountains fringing the road each side, and the nothingness unfurls in front of you like a big hazy carpet for about 60 miles. It's sort of beautiful, in a desolate way, but after a bit, it starts messing with your head. And this is just the start.

Fortunately, distractions don't come any more distracting than a lime-green Lamborghini packing 552bhp. Cops with itchy trigger fingers and radar are an ever-present threat out here, but sitting in sixth gear at 65mph for the next 200 miles is clearly not an option. So with the signal from the obligatory classic rock station fading, I start playing tunes with the Lambo's exhaust instead.

Pavarotti's spirit must have moved into the manifold. Even in sixth with about 4,000rpm showing on the rev counter, a little throttle tickle elicits a great barrel-chested roar that swells into a feral howl as you close in on the red line. This sort of thing is part of an Italian supercar's job description, but the LP560's V10 sounds better than most.

Like everyone else, Lambo insists the automated manual is the way forward. I insist it isn't, even if 90 per cent of Gallardo buyers opt for the 'e-gear' transmission. The new car's 'box has been completely redesigned, and it's now lighter and comes with five different shift maps (including the potentially ruinous 'Thrust' mode for showing off).

The shift time has apparently been cut from a positively glacial 210m/s to 120m/s, which is still some way off the pace. It remains fairly agricultural in feel, though that's not necessarily a bad thing. Apparently, Lamborghini's customers prefer a more 'emotional' experience, which is to say a jerky, mechanical shift versus the seamless action you get in the latest dual-clutch transmissions.

By the time we've 'crossed the hump to Pahrump', as the locals like to say, the temperature has risen from 23 to 33°C. Pahrump is the last proper town – fast-food joints, churches, malls, billboards promoting lawyers and vasectomies and lawyers who can handle bungled vasectomies – before Death Valley. There is genuine tumbleweed and dust.

At the crossroads of the 127 and 190 highways, we arrive at Death Valley Junction, established in the 1920s by the Pacific Coast Borax Company. It's 43°C outside, but the LP560 is coping perfectly. Now the car really does look like something from another planet. In fact, right now *this* planet looks like something from another planet. We press on; the Lambo feels more muscular than ever, more tangibly macho than the occasionally highly strung Ferrari F430 or bullish Aston Martin Vantage.

Dante's View, the top of which crests 5,475ft, contrasts starkly with Badwater; at 282ft below sea level, it's not only the lowest point in North America but also a Precambrian geological marvel, which means it's been doing its thing for about 1.8 billion years. Zabriskie Point, celebrated in Antonioni's counter-cultural 1970 film classic and featured on the cover of U2's *Joshua Tree*, is even more mind-blowing (and younger too, at a mere 65 million years).

All told, there are 3.3 million acres to choose from in Death Valley, including a surprising number of corners. With four-wheel drive, and shod in new low-rolling-resistance Pirelli P Zeroes, the Gallardo is blessed with other-worldly levels of grip and balance. Ferrari's F430 is ultimately more adjustable, and a little easier to slide if that's what you're after, but the Gallardo's speed and composure through fast corners is little short of phenomenal. Great steering too; some small refinements mean it's now less likely to kick back in your hands when the surface beneath the wheels turns nasty. It's even comfortable.

In fact, this is a truly great car. Lamborghini has almost always produced *great-looking* cars, but with the Gallardo LP560, 45 years of epic potential has finally been fulfilled. Yes, it'll do 202mph and accelerate to 62mph in 3.7 seconds. And yes, it has weapons-grade looks, and eats corners for breakfast. But as we turn round, settle into a sixth-gear cruise, and head back into civilisation – well, Las Vegas anyway – something awful dawns on me.

This bad boy isn't very bad at all. It's very good. 🔳

Expect to find a Russian wideboy trussed up in D&G behind the wheel

A perfect

Story by Paul Horrell, Photography by Lee Brimble

storm

Alfa's 8C Competizione captures the rawness and romance of a Romeo. But does this supercar signal a new tradition for the marque or is it simply a brief, beautiful storm?

FASHION IS A SLIPPERY BUGGER. THE moment you allow yourself to think you've got a hold of it, it flies out of your hands like a bar of soap. Classical beauty lasts longer, and Alfa must be glad of this, for here they are launching a car first shown four whole years ago. If the 8C Competizione's styling had been tied to the ship of fashion back then, it'd be wrecked on some forgotten coast by now.

Luckily it wasn't. It was, and remains, knee-tremblingly gorgeous in the time-honoured manner of an Italian front-engined two-seater. Just how gorgeous was hard to appreciate when we only ever glimpsed it in sections at motor shows, the majority of its form always occluded by the close-pressed palpitating flesh of car-loving humanity. But now it's out in the open and ready to roll, the answer is *entirely* gorgeous.

It was designed by Wolfgang Egger, then Alfa design boss, now at Audi. At the time of the concept car he told me it was 'modern, but with tradition,' when I asked him if it was too retro. It harks back to the era of coachbuilt track-biased Alfas. "We remembered the 2000 Sportiva, the 33 Stradale and the TZ." Holy cow, they were good things to remember. It has the long, high nose and short teardrop cabin of the TZ, and the extraordinarily beautiful surface curves of the 33 Stradale.

Which is all well and good, but I do have some reservations about this car. Let's get them out of the way, eh, so we can end on a high note. For a start, look at the name: 8C Competizione. The 8C is easy – eight cylinders, reflecting honestly a long-time Alfa designation. But Competizione: where's the racing? The looks reflect old Alfa racers, yes, and it's made partly of carbon. But it's not a semi-racer. It's a road car, built for style and Sunday morning blasts. That's OK, so why give it a travesty of a name?

Maybe the dishonesty of the word Competizione was OK on a concept car, which is how it started out all those years ago. Such a clamour of adoration built up around it that Alfa started to look at production. But before long, parent company Fiat was in such deep do-do that they couldn't contemplate anything so wildly non-core.

Then Fiat healed itself, and the project was back on, engineered to this state in just 18 months.

But it remains non-core, a V8 supercar that's triple the price of anything else Alfa does. A halo car, you say? Well yes, it'll score Alfa some attention as it goes back to the USA in 2009. The 8C is a seriously enticing machine, but it doesn't really advance the art of the supercar. And frankly I can't help wishing they'd put these engineers onto finessing the Brera a bit. Still, to be fair, I always had the same reservations about the irrelevance of the Ford GT, and I have to admit I was in the minority. Enough musing. Let's drive.

So you get in, itching to go. But you don't go anywhere, at least for a few minutes. Because you're paralysed by the extraordinary world you find yourself in. The cabin is beautiful and to me even better than the outside, because it's more inventive, more progressive and yet even more identifiably Italian. The seats have supercar bolstering, but they're covered in a wonderful woven leather. The bits that look like aluminium are exactly that. In fact they're machined from solid, so for each car they start with 100 kilos of metal and end up with 5kg of switches and doorhandles and 95kg of swarf. Meanwhile the dash and console are naked carbon fibre. This has more to do with it being cheap to tool-up for a low-volume hand-built machine than with it having anything to do with a racetrack, but the material shimmers seductively in the Northern Italian morning sunlight.

Press a starter button. It's answered by a lengthy ring of starter motor. Just as you're thinking it'll never fire, you get punched in the chest by an explosion of V8 tailpipe lunacy. This is one aristocratic engine. It's made by Ferrari, related to the Maserati unit of the Quattroporte, and GranTurismo, but instead of 4.2 litres it's 4.7, and so gets an extra 50bhp. That makes 450. Blip the throttle and it sounds that number. At the very least.

The 8C isn't made for dawdling but it will trickle along without reluctance: at low revs, if you stay off the throttle the noise is kept somewhere the sociable side of outrage, and it's possible to persuade the paddleshifted transaxle automated-manual gearbox ⁝

1. Those knobs are milled from solid aluminium. Quality

2. Red leather interior oozes Italian sex appeal and style

3. Sleek styling extends to the trio of headlights

1.

2.

3.

'The Alfa 8C is gorgeous. Just how gorgeous was hard to appreciate when we glimpsed it at motor shows. Now, out in the open, it is *entirely* gorgeous'

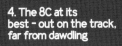

4.

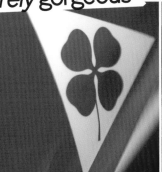

5.

4. The 8C at its best – out on the track, far from dawdling

5. Change down a gear or two, just to hear the exhaust pop

6. Only 500 8Cs will be built. Er, when does ours arrive?

1. Paddle-shifters look a seamless part of the steering wheel

2. A gentle reminder of which exclusive car you're driving

3. 100kg of aluminium gave its life to create this lovely interior

'When the needle swings beyond 4,000 there's a really sharp step in the force, and another one at about 6,000, where the 8C's pants really catch alight

4. Engine boasts 450bhp and a 0-60 time of 4.2secs

5. Italian? Check. Two-seater? Check. Gorgeous? Check

6. Forget everything else. The 8C has wheels to die for

into moderately soft-edged shifts. But once you start work on the accelerator, delicious sonic craziness is all yours. It's distinctive, too, with a lot more bass in the mix than a Ferrari, but with the edgy top-notes intact. You can make it woofle, you can make it scream. And when it is screaming, the noise echoes its way around the hard-surfaced cabin for maximum effect. This is in no way a peaceful tourer.

So while we're at it, let's press the sport button on the console. Normally there's a valve to muffle the exhaust a little below 4,000rpm. Sport mode locks this out. It also quickens the throttle pedal travel, shortens gearchange times and gives you extra leeway on the ESP threshold.

So with 450bhp cracking away at 1,585kg, it's fast. Fast in that highly-tuned naturally-aspirated way: you have to go and fetch the power from the far end of the rev-counter, so you're staying with the car, tipping the paddles at the just-so moment, stoking the red-hot fire ahead. When the needle swings beyond 4,000 there's a really sharp step in the force, and another one – less significant but still enticing – at about 6,000, from where the 8C's pants properly catch alight and it charges for the 7,500rpm red-line as if that were the only place to find an extinguisher. Oh and when you change down a gear, there's a succession of pops and cackles from the exhaust, like devilish laughter. It doesn't spit flame, but you just know it should. The figures look like this: 0-62mph in 4.2 seconds and 183mph.

That's not all. After a few miles you're in thrall to the fact that this is more, far more, than a powertrain car.

The Maserati Cambiocorsa gearbox is at the back, and weight distribution is slightly rear-biased. And though it uses Quattroporte suspension, the wheelbase is significantly shorter than any Maser on sale now, the subframes are bolted solidly to the body instead of through bushes, the steering rack is more direct, the springs and anti-roll bars are stiffer, and the dampers don't bother with the wobbly and ineffective Skyhook adaptive nonsense – they're in the tensed-and-ready position all the time. There are 20-inch P Zeroes, 285-35 section at the back, and downforce thanks to an underfloor venturi.

So it was built to handle. They could afford to make the springs stiff because they've got a very stiff body to mount them to. The screen pillars, roof, aft pillars and rear wings are a single carbon lay-up, providing huge stiffness. The front wings, door skins and bonnet are carbon too, for lightness. The upper carbon structure is bonded to a steel lower platform, borrowed from the Quattroporte again but shortened and modified.

It works. Well, it does on home turf at least. Alfa is letting outsiders drive it only at the company's own Balocco test track (boo hiss), but it's a long and interesting circuit and I'm having a ball. The 8C is confident and balanced, and grippy as anything. Of course it understeers on very tight bends if you go in too fast, so the right way is to be cautious on the way in and incautious with the throttle on the way out. Kill the ESP and it's a real drifter. In faster stuff, it's reassuring but balanced and very much alive. The brake pedal has an overly long travel and on this glassy-smooth surface it was hard to judge how much steering feel there was, but I suspect not as much as the best of this world's mid- and rear-engined cars. But when you think about Astons and AMG SLs and M6s and Corvettes, I'd say the 8C is more fun.

It should be. For a start it's ruddy expensive at £111,000. Two, the set-up doesn't leave much room for comfort. It slaps hard onto bumps, even things like manhole covers. But on the other hand, once the bump has gone, it's really history. The related Quattroporte gets all wrapped up in shuddering and aftershocks. The Alfa just deals with it. That's partly because the carbon-and-steel body is so stiff.

We mustn't be too kind to the 8C Competizione. It always feels like the rushed job it is, in the sense that it hasn't had the rough edges painstakingly worked off like a 911 Turbo or even a Gallardo has. But in the right circumstance, that's what makes it special. Alfa is being canny keeping it as a limited edition, with just 41 coming to Britain out of a world total of 500. Every one is sold. Ah well, before long they'll announce a fresh run of a spider version, so if you want to be part of that hysteria, make yourself known to Alfa now.

LIMITED RUN

THE 599XX IS A SECOND OFF FXX PACE, HAS 700BHP AND WEIGHS 1,330KG.
THERE'S JUST ONE DOWNSIDE – YOU CAN ONLY DRIVE IT WHEN FERRARI SAYS SO

WORDS: TOM FORD PHOTOGRAPHY: JOE WINDSOR-WILLIAMS

+ The rear-light
clusters are
replaced by vents
in the 599XX

+ Carbon fibre –
super light and
looks like an optical
illusion too. Wow

MONEY, THEY SAY, won't make you happy. But it will get you much better toys, which make you *happier*. And *Top Gear* can't think of much better toy than this 599XX. A properly cranked-up gentleman-racer variant of the most complete supercar in the world.

The only slight dirty little fly in the Rosso Corsa ointment is that the 599XX will only ever be a toy, because this headbanger is not a road car, and never will be. Nor is it a full-on raceable competition car. It's being sold with the same caveats as the Ferrari FXX: track-use only as part of a development programme run by Ferrari itself. Basically, you pony-up 1.1million euro and become a Ferrari test driver, with one of only 15 599XXs thrown in as the world's most impressive track-day car-cum-garage ornament.

For that shall we say, fairly unsubtle sum, you get to become part of the Ferrari 'family' and have Ferrari technicians forensically dissect your lap times to discover just how rubbish your driving really is, while they gather myriad data about how

to improve their future high performance cars. A new system called 'Virtual Car Engineer' provides a screen in the car that provides a real-time indication of the car's efficiency, and therefore where you're going wrong. There will be no place to hide. As with the FXX, you'll get to play at 15 of the world's most famous circuits over a period of two years (with the car run by the Ferrari mechanics) and possibly contribute to the scientific development of future technology.

But that all seems a bit by-the-by when you take a look at the spec of the 599XX – this is not a brief tweak and some fancy spoilers. Although the 599XX is based on the 599 Fiorano, the engineers have been playing silly buggers with virtually every aspect of the car. The headlines are impressive enough, with the re-engineer of the Fiorano's V12 now producing 700bhp at an eye-popping 9,000rpm.

They've managed the power and fizz increase by reducing internal friction and shaving weight from internal components so the car revs more freely, and then adopting a flurry of exotic bits'n'bobs for the rest – the intake plenums, for example, are now made of pure carbon fibre. And what hasn't been wrought from unobtainium has been deleted or made lighter: there are Lexan windows, no power ⸪

motors for any of the interior accoutrements, a significant lack of the comfy stuff.

The gearbox has also been re-engineered, and free from the comfort and useability constraints of a road-biased car has now dropped shift times to just 60 milliseconds – much less than the proverbial blink of an eye. This thing will be brutal. But Ferrari still reckons that it will be quite a different experience to the FXX – more a GT racer than the F1-commitment of the Enzo-based car.

Customers will, Ferrari hopes, spend more time in the car when it doesn't try and bite your head off quite so hard. Then again, even though no performance times have been published, the 599XX weighs just 1,330kg (some 330kg less than the stock car) and laps Ferrari's Fiorano test track within one second of the FXX and 10 seconds faster than the road version. This should not be considered a 'soft' option.

Probably of more interest to Ferrari is the aerodynamic package that includes some real-deal features that might have more direct technological trickle-down than the lonely drip from the rarefied heights of F1. A new system called 'Actiflow' can increase downforce or decrease drag depending on conditions thanks to a new porous material in the diffuser (it looks like pumice stone) and two fans in the boot that channel airflow from under the car out through two vents replacing the rear lights. You may think this stuff is unlikely to make it to a road car, but the grilles in the rear of the 430 Scud that vent

the high pressure from inside the wheel arch (reducing rear-end lift) come directly from a system used on the FXX project. It's nearer than you think.

The rest of the aerodynamics are more traditional, but no less effective: the combination of big spoiler, winglets, a flat underbody and other tweaks mean that the 599XX produces 280kg of real downforce at 120mph and a not-inconsiderable 630kg at 185mph. There are even F1-derived 'doughnuts' which partly cover the carbon brake discs and wheel rim, smoothing the airflow around the wheels and helping regulate the brake temperature. Slap on the standard slicks and you'll be good to go.

Ferrari is being canny here. The FXX project demonstrated that they could get a partial bankroll for R&D by the very people that are likely to buy their future cars. The people that get involved in the 599XX programme (as with the FXX) are likely to be very passionate about their driving and therefore better than average, but they also provide invaluable information about how a high-end Ferrari customer wants their car to feel. Japanese mega-rich people, for example, prefer totally different things than customers in North America or Europe.

The only other thing to remember is that if you buy into the 599XX programme you can't just sell the car. Ferrari has first refusal on the sale, simply because you're not just buying a vehicle, you're buying into a development package. Ferrari wants to make sure it knows exactly who gets to influence future product. Nice work if you can afford it. 🔟

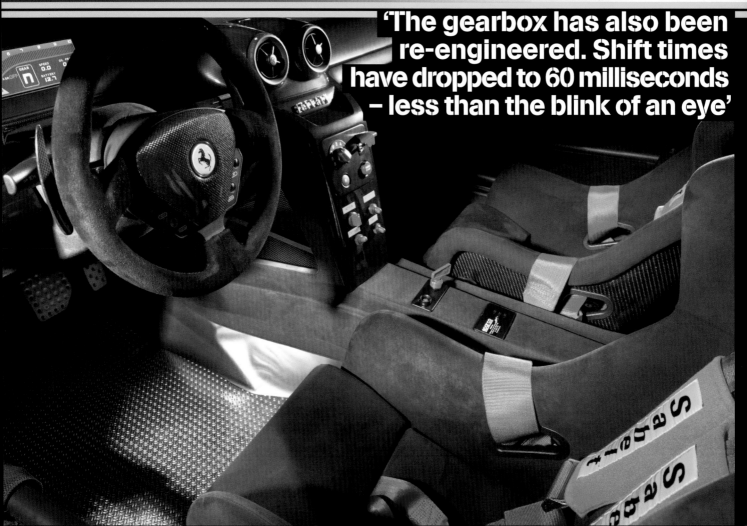

'The gearbox has also been re-engineered. Shift times have dropped to 60 milliseconds – less than the blink of an eye'

Buy one of these and be involved in the development of future Ferraris

Disappointing it only goes up to 9, we'd like to turn it up to 11...

Winglets make the move from last season's F1 cars to 'proper' cars. Kinda

Worries that Ferrari might have
adulterated its sports heritage with
the California prove to be needless;
this is one red hot chilli pepper

Califor

Words by Tom Ford Photography by Lee Brimble

nication

THE FIRST TIME I CATCH SIGHT OF THE NEW California, it's parked slightly askew on a wide swathe of concrete, roof down, with heat haze making the air go all treacly and slow over the light blue bonnet, giving it a slightly mirage-style vibe. For at least five minutes, I just stare. This car has a *lot* of stuff going on, a big, noisy eye-party that can force your brain into neutral with the sheer number of slats, scoops, slashes and strakes. I realise that my jaw has been hanging brain-dead slack for a couple of minutes, and snap it shut with an audible pop as a Ferrari employee saunters up, quite obviously deciding that my stunned appearance is due to the car's sheer, heart-fumbling beauty.

"So, Tom, you like it, eh?" he says with the kind of warm threat that only Italians can properly manage.

"I, uh... I...", I flap, struggling to find the appropriate response. My eyes track down at the generously proportioned rump and the swathe of ultra plastic-looking black plastic that frames the rear 'plate and announce, "It looks different in pictures, and, well, I kind of like the, er... front bit. With the thing on. The scoop. I *like* scoops..."

Clearly pleased with my incisive breakdown of the delicate nuances of the car's design, Ferrari man moves on. As he wanders off, my mouth drops open again, and stays that way for about 15 minutes.

No instant attraction here, then, more raised eyebrows and pursed-lips and gawping. It's not a pretty car in the traditional sense, especially with the roof stowed, where the necessity of hiding the roof sections swells the rear to, ahem, generous proportions. A size eight car with a size 12 arse. The car is also quite big, bigger than you might imagine at 5cm longer than an F430, and more like the 599 than you think it will be. Which is no bad thing. Roof up, there's more cohesion, more lusty sportiness, and it slims the whole car down by giving your eye a line to follow, rather than having it always attracted to the stump of the rump. Saying that, the longer you spend with it, the more it grows on you – you pick up more of the little details every time you move 10 degrees. I particularly like the little inverted swoosh that tries to draw your eye away from the high-ish waisted rear, and exposure allows it to gel in your head more firmly. More so when you step inside and start to discover what the California is really all about.

Now, I'd heard plenty about what the California was 'supposed' to be. The baby Ferrari. The more accessible Ferrari. The Ferrari for people who want a Ferrari, but don't want a mid-engined application for wankerdom. You may appreciate the hell out of an F430, but the British mindset is that if you buy a mid-engined Ferrari, you're a bit nouveau and definitely a bit flash. So the California, despite all the exterior ostentation, gets a more rational, more GT focus than hardcore sports-

car arrangement. It has a 340-litre boot that drops to a still-pretty-good 240 litres with the roof stowed, for goodness' sake. You could use this during the week, as well as at weekends. So, think of it more like a 612 in vibe than a 599 or F430.

So, the basics are that there's a new direct-injection 4.3-litre V8 motor mounted up front, though its probably mounted far back enough to really be classed as front-mid-engined, driving the rear wheels. The car weighs 1735kg, seats two in comfort and four in an almost entirely theoretical sense. As per any Ferrari in living memory, only the rear wheels are driven, aided by F1-Trac traction and 'CST' stability control and a three-position (rather than the five positions on the F430) 'mannetino' dial to switch between Comfort, Sport and CST-off. That little box of transmission, suspension and traction-control-altering tricks is mounted on the right-hand side of the steering wheel. You start the engine by hitting the brake pedal and prodding the big red 'engine start' on the bottom left. And then all the good stuff starts happening at once, and the California starts to look a whole lot more tasty.

The all-aluminium engine itself produces 454bhp, 357lb ft of torque and revs to 8,000rpm. It gets to 62mph in 'under four seconds' according to Ferrari and will hit 193mph. Which blatantly aren't statistics that you'd associate with some sort of Ferrari-Lite. It channels the power via a new Getrag-fettled seven-speed double-clutch gearbox – a first on a Ferrari – the big news being this offers an F1-style shift with an auto mode that actually works. Properly, without burning out a clutch

I'd heard plenty about what the California was "supposed" to be. The baby Ferrari. The more accessible Ferrari'

in one three-point turn. You feel it as soon as you pull away, there's none of the slightly fluffy moving-off response of the more aggressive F1, even though the cues (paddles, buttons etc.) are all the same. Let's face it, 599-style robotised F1 gearboxes are a joy when going hard, but can't manage a smooth auto mode. To defeat the nodding-dog syndrome when changing gears, you end up short-shifting the paddles in any case.

The open road, an open top and, just round the corner, certain death

Ceramic brakes pull the Cali to a gurning stop, thankfully

'The California is living up to the brief: easy to drive, comfortable, and it feels, dare I say it, civilised'

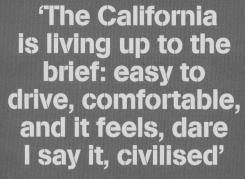

Ferrari grille looks a lot like the mouth of a basking shark

For the ultimate in feedback and feel, place your hands here

So I start feel pretty positive as we listen to a 'proper' Ferrari burble-cum-bark pootling out to some open countryside. The California is living up to the brief: comfortable, easy to drive, and it feels, dare I say it, more civilised than any Ferrari before it. It's not intimidating. Which, for a while, I can't decide whether or not is a good thing. Still, press the 'auto' button mounted on the silvery spar of a centre console to knock the self-shifting on the head, drop a couple of gears via the left hand paddle, shift into 'Sport' on the mannetino and floor it, and your brain bulges sideways through your ears with the acceleration, only to be pushed back in by a noise that feels like it's going to tear something sticky but important free inside your head. Three gears in, and you're done wondering – this is still a Ferrari, no question. Noise, fury, neck-snapping street presence, steering that, although it can bobble a bit on really lumpy roads, loves to whisper sweet everything into your brain via your palms.

But after about an hour searching out some decent roads here in sunny Sicily, that noise becomes a point of contention on the autostrada. With the roof down, it is really very loud – great at first, slightly wearing after a while – especially as the new gearbox has a habit, in auto mode, of hanging onto seventh gear for as long as the torque curve will stand it and then launching back into fourth, causing the engine to plop straight into noise-maker mode. Possibly good for emissions standards; bad when you really want to slip by unnoticed. In town, it looks like you're doing it on purpose, which isn't quite as stealth as you might like. With the roof up, the noise is just fine, perfect for a little windows-down tunnel-running, but not intrusive when you just want to get somewhere, and talk to a passenger while doing it. Still, I reckon someone eyeing up a Merc SL63 will think the California is very shouty indeed at low speed. Actually, I'll rephrase that; they're going to think the California is just very shouty.

I'd love to tell you that I then took the California out and found that the chassis was a complete delight. And I can, but only up to a point. Basically, while Sicilian roads are great for ascertaining that the California's standard suspension (you can get an adjustable magneto-rheological damper set-up as an option) is really very good at soaking up lots of bumps without shaking the steering or your bingo wings too much, it's almost bloody useless about telling you how much grip is ultimately available. Road-mending, apart from the rather lovely new stretches of autostrada, appears to be a forgotten art. The roads appear to be constructed of a special concrete that, when exposed to more than a year of salt and sun, take on the grip characteristics of oiled grey glass. Apply rubber tyres to said surface, especially tyres with 450-odd bhp to contend with, and even the very merest twitch of your right foot will see the car trying to step – albeit serenely – sideways.

Hence, despite having at once the most amusingly slithery drive and the most financially fear-racked driving experience of my entire life (£145k and cliff edges – and steady hands are not always my speciality), I can't tell you much about serious on-the-limit handling and grip levels. Though it is possible to say with some conviction that it feels beautifully balanced – if it weren't, I'd be writing this from a Sicilian fracture clinic and photographer Brimble wouldn't be sending me a Christmas card this year. Luckily, the standard CCM carbon-ceramic brakes, which shed a helpful 15kg from the overall weight of the California versus trad steel stoppers, can pull the car up without fuss or fade from pretty much any speed. And they're feelsome too, which helps when you fear that you're about to spear a retaining wall and then literally head into the harbour. What shines through, though – despite Sicily's best attempts to hide it – is the fact that the California is still, even with the attempt at GT-ness, a very focussed car. That Mercedes SL ⸫

we were talking about? Well, despite being more of a driver's car in the current generation, it can't come close to the California. Ditto the Bentley GTC. The Aston comes closer, a Porsche Turbo Cab even more so, but neither feel anywhere near as encouraging, and so wantonly vocal about it.

And the DSG makes you want to play with the performance, stretch the car into all sorts of interesting places. It's not the same experience as you might imagine if you've driven a dual-clutch on say, a German car like a TT or a Porsche. Where they feel slightly synthetic, the Ferrari system has a kick. It recovers kinetic energy from the engine to accelerate the gearchange itself, added some added elasticity, some extra 'boing' to the gearchange moment. Where a Porsche PDK feels like the ultimate sports-car version of the S-Tronic TT, the Ferrari feels like an F1 'box with even quicker changes and some added civility. And though there is no obvious step-change in gearbox reaction speed when you switch from comfort to sport like there is in a traditional F1 'box, the escalation of the traction-control threshold almost makes you think there is.

You'll still find yourself visiting 8,000rpm and snapping through a couple of gears for no other reason than it makes you feel really good about driving a car like this. There doesn't have to be a point. If you like things loud, crackling and electrifying, it becomes the point.

So, despite hefty misgivings at the start, I have to say that Ferrari has cracked it. There are bits I don't like – some of the plastics around the rear end look wrong on such an expensive car, and the rear is about 10 per cent too hefty-looking. But for that, you get a coupe and convertible that can swap closed for open in just 15 seconds and manages to look pretty damn good in either guise. Think about it; coupe/convertibles are usually pretty obvious about their transforming abilities. Apart from the SL, a CC usually telegraphs itself. Here it doesn't so much. And what Ferrari has managed to do is create a car that isn't as intimidating as any of its other automotive speed-seekers, isn't as keen to slap you down if you get things marginally wrong, is easier to drive, easier to live with, more flexible, and it has done it without making it an Italian clone of something else. This is a proper, God's honest, marrow-deep Ferrari – it just comes in a different, more subtle flavour.

But the best bit? This is still a car that will make you laugh out loud and put a smile on your face broad enough to hurt your cheeks. Which, at the end of the day, is all we can ask for. And all we ever wanted.

'The rear end is about
10 per cent too hefty-
looking. But you do get
a coupe/convertible
that can swap closed
for open in just
15 seconds'

There is

And the 430 Scuderia is indeed God's own supercar. As you know, **Jeremy Clarkson** doesn't fall in love lightly. But this is different

a GOD

Photography by Lee Brimble

W HEN A COUPLE DECIDES to get married, it is the job of the bride and her family to organise the church, the party, the dress, the invitations, the catering, the vicar, the bridesmaids, the cars, the present list and the vast quantity of beer needed to quench the thirst of the New Zealanders who turn up to build the marquee.

The bridegroom, on the other hand, must busy himself choosing a nice place to go on honeymoon.

There are many remote islands from which to choose. You've got the Maldives, Mauritius, the Seychelles and Tahiti, long before you even arrive at the Caribbean where the choice becomes even more bewildering and complex.

The brochures are no help. Because I know for a fact that they all use exactly the same shot of exactly the same palm tree no matter what island paradise they're talking about. But don't worry, because while the travel people are useless, Uncle Jeremy can help...

Having been to most of these places, I can assure you that they are all exactly the same. You'll have a white beach, blue sea, and an endless array of men in silly costumes who'll endeavour to make your life as pleasant as possible. Usually by bringing your breakfast to your room on something hugely inappropriate. Like an elephant. Or a canoe.

It is much the same story with supercars. Oh, you may dream about a Maserati, but you know what? When all is said and done, it'll do almost exactly the same job as any of the others. Get you noticed and move you much more quickly than is sensible or prudent. While bellowing.

Happily, however, unlike honeymoon hideaways, there is one exception with supercars. One brand that does stand out: Ferrari. It doesn't matter whether you're talking about the 430, the 599 or the 612 – they feel very different to the rest of the breed. They feel... better.

It's hard to explain why. Ferrari blathers on about the e-diffs and the variable valves and the stupid manettino switch on the steering wheel, but none of this has anything to do with it. It's hard, even, to describe the feeling in words, but I always imagine when I'm in a Ferrari that they feel like other cars will feel in about 20 years' time.

They have a lightness and delicacy you don't get in other supercars. There's a poise too, and a sense in your buttocks, ears and fingertips that all will be well no matter how fast you entered the last bend. I like driving them... a lot.

But I don't want to own one, partly because they are not pretty enough, but mainly because the passion and the love and the soul that made Ferraris so special in the past is sort of buried under all the technology. You don't feel like you're in a painting. You feel like you're in a digital photograph. ⊰

'Ferraris have a lightness and delicacy you don't get in other supercars. And they give you a sense in your butt that all will be well, no matter how fast you drive'

DH 664 YT

F430 Scud provides the filth and the fury of an old school Ferrari

Trad Ferrari dials with an 80s vibe. But no Magnum motor, this one

There's been more stripping in here than in your average Spearmint Rhino

That riotous V8 makes an exhibition of itself at the rear

'The upshot is 503bhp in a full-on fury car that weighs 100kg less than the standard version. And, boy, can you sense this on the road'

Ceramic brakes in 430 are far more progressive than in McMerc SLR. Outstanding

The new Scuderia though... ooh, that's a different story.

In recent months, we've seen a lightweight Lamborghini Gallardo and a lightweight Porsche GT3. and if we're honest, they are only marginally better than the standard cars. But a lot more expensive.

The Scud is a lot more expensive than the standard car as well. At £172,500, it's £28k more expensive in fact. And for this you get no radio, no carpets, less soundproofing, welds that appear to have been done by apes, carbon fibre where you'd expect something more substantial and a few body tweaks that make the already not very pretty body a bit more slippery. And worse.

Things you can't see? Well it has titanium springs, carbon ceramic brakes, modified pistons, a revised exhaust system, 20bhp more from the 4.3-litre V8, and yet another setting on the stupid manettino steering wheel switch which lets you drive with the stability control on, but the traction control off.

Bollocks. You are either on the road, in which case you want the dampers in their soft setting, and everything on. Or you are on a track, in which case you want the suspension firmed up and everything else off. Who needs five degrees of difference, for crying out loud?

Could it be, perhaps, this is a car aimed at ghastly track-day enthusiasts whose wives hate them? Certainly the idiotic four-point racing harnesses would suggest this to be so. Why would they be fitted otherwise? No really. All they say to me is: "You're going to have a crash so enormous, a normal seatbelt and an airbag won't be able to save you."

No matter. The upshot is 503bhp in a full-on fury car that weighs a full 100kg less than the standard version. And boy can you sense this on the road where it is unbelievably, staggeringly, joyously noisy. This is the one sensation you take away above all the others. The noise. The drone. The headache.

You are dimly aware of some speed, and surprisingly compliant suspension. You vaguely register the speed of the flappy paddle gearbox and how smoothly it changes these days. And then you have to have another Nurofen.

I loved it. I loved it because here was a Ferrari that drove like a Ferrari *and* had the passion of a Ferrari as well. It felt raw, and crude and dirty. It felt like its favourite item of clothing would be a mac, and that if you parked it up in suburbia, it would steal women's underwear from their washing lines and peep at all the housewives while they were showering.

And that's before I showed it a track, where it got better and better. I still maintain a flappy paddle gearbox doesn't work in everyday use – *you* try to parallel park on a hill – but in the Ferrari, on a track, the changes are so quick you don't feel them.

And then there's the braking. When I first tried carbon ceramic discs, just three years ago, on a McLaren Mercedes, I thought they were a silly spin off from Formula 1 that either squeaked if you used them gently, or hurled you through the windscreen if you were a bit more firm. Not any more. In the Scuderia, they stop you fast, and with feel, and endlessly. They are brilliant.

And so's the engine. Maybe there's a small torque hole in the standard car's V8, but there isn't in the Scuderia. It's a wall of power – and sound – all the way up to 8,700rpm.

And through the bends? Well it feels like a standard 430 – which is the highest praise – only a bit better, a bit livelier, a bit more willing to change direction. Apparently, it's so grippy that it can generate 1.5g. That's incredible.

Ferrari says that round its race track, the new car is quicker than an Enzo. Hmmm. Ferrari says that every new car they ever launch is quicker than everything else they've ever made. It is not as quick as an Enzo and that's an end of it. It does 0 to 60 in 3.6 seconds and does only 199 flat out. But it's much, much nicer to drive.

Yes, there's computer stuff. The e-diff talks to the traction system behind your back, for instance, but you feel part of the machine – you feel like you're in something created by enthusiasts, not technicians.

As you cannon out of a bend, marvelling at the wall of sound and the extraordinary grip, you are pinned in your seat, unaware that the ride height is down, or that the air is being parted more cleanly. All you care about is that you don't want it to stop.

As a driving machine, I know of nothing to match this. With a radio – a loud one, so you could hear it – a better looking body and proper seatbelts, it would be just about perfect.

With a honeymoon island, life is easy. Just pick the nearest. And the cheapest. With supercars, it's even easier. Just pick a 430 Scuderia. **TG**

+ F430 Scuderia graces the *Top Gear* studio with its presence

Ger

many

A land of precision, of engineering perfection, where pride is taken in every last nut and bolt. But don't make the mistake of assuming the Germans have less passion than the Italians when it comes to supercars.

One visit to Affalterbach, home of AMG, makes a mockery of that theory. Here you'll find some of the most gifted, hard-working and yes, passionate car-makers on the planet. And the spirit they pour into their cars is as unfiltered as the Italians'. Same for Zuffenhausen, home of Porsche. The place names don't quite stir the emotion in the same way as those in Italy, but the cars certainly do.

Audi is taking a big gamble with its first supercar, the R8.
But after his first drive, Paul Horrell thinks it's worth a flutter

Photography by Mark Bramley

High
Roller

'On roads you don't know, through corners you haven't learned, over poor or unpredictable surfaces, the R8 is on your side, like no other mid-engined car'

It's the same powerplant as in the RS4, exposed for all to stare at

How novel, a gearknob that doubles as a microphone

SINCE THE FIRST R8 PHOTOS LAST summer there's been a feeling abroad that this car deserves a good kicking. People are arguing that the cold rationality of Ingolstadt doesn't translate into the emotional realm of the supercar. Word is the R8 doesn't have the right aura of specialness or drama. And that Audi anyway is misguided even trying to sell a car like this because people who buy £77,000 supercars want supercar badges.

There's a more sinister undercurrent too. In a decade, Audi has swept from the sympathetic position of left-field underdog to dominating several market sectors and a race series, and done it with a ruthlessness that's very unattractive. So people have stopped rooting for Audi and by extension turned against its customers, as a scan of the *TG* blogosphere will show. The mood is implicit but pervasive: let the Audi backlash begin.

Well, sorry people, but I can't think of a worse way to approach a new supercar. I'm a pragmatist and I want to know what the R8 does for the driver. Do its go/stop/steer departments properly float my boat? How do its cockpit and external design work on the road? If it's a good car, all the rest – a position for Audi in the sports-car pantheon, a more generous-spirited view of its styling and of its drivers – will surely follow.

So, with the keys to an R8 in my hand and a range of mountains in the near-distance, beyond which is a conveniently opened racetrack, I am of the view that the time for chin-stroking theorising is past. Let's drive!

There's drama even as you drop into the seat. This isn't an exquisite conventional coupe cockpit like an Aston Vantage or even a non-exquisite but perfectly executed one like a 911's. It's a supercar, low and wide. The seat is the optional sports bucket that hugs you so tight it's almost embarrassing. Surrounding you is another bit of furniture to fetishise your inner race fantasist. The so-called 'monoposto' evokes the outline of a single seater's cockpit, a hoop that arches up either side of your knees and over the instruments. Yes it's contrived, but it's harmless fun and maybe stops you noticing that most of the switchgear is lifted straight out of the TT. Not that that's bad stuff in itself, but the R8 is supposed to be extraordinary.

At first I'm wondering how extraordinary the performance truly is. The feeling is slightly understated, for three reasons, I reckon. First, the throttle response is just ever-so-slightly soft. In a supercar I want to feel that tickling the throttle is releasing a caged animal, but here you have to rouse it. Secondly, the engine is so well-developed there's no kick-point in the torque curve, and the absence of troughs means the peak doesn't feel so high. Thirdly, in the name of making this a civilised everyday supercar, they've neutered the exhaust from inside the cabin. It sounds good, but not quite great. Paradoxically, for lucky bystanders the V8's tailpipes rumble like those in *Talladega Nights*. Wind down the window.

Still, floor it and you'd best be paying attention. It'll out-accelerate a 911 C4S. This is the RS4's 4.2-litre direct-injection V8, but with a dry sump, so it can sit lower in the car. It makes 414bhp at 7,200, and goes on to a searing 8,250. That, coupled with Araldite traction, kicks you to 62mph in 4.6secs, to 125mph in 14.9secs, and on to 187mph. So it's properly quick.

Through the mountains, good news keeps coming. On roads you don't know, through corners you haven't learned, over poor or unpredictable surfaces, the R8 is on your side like no other mid-engined car. That's a priceless virtue. The steering isn't all that high-geared, so you use definite movements and get definite, positive, predictable results. No, there isn't quite the feedback of a 911 'wheel, but what you get instead is a wonderful sense that the front of the car is planted into the road. Peel it hard into a slow corner and there's a little stabilising understeer, but use a little throttle and it settles neutrally, before an awesome catapult exit. Back off and it'll tuck the nose in too, but ever so benignly. In faster curves it's solid and true. It swallows bumps and hardly rolls. The body control is terrific.

And yet it rides beautifully. I've got the optional magnetic-fluid adaptive dampers, and they do a great job of filtering out shudders. The aluminium bodyshell feels rock-rigid too. You're strapped into a piece of real precision engineering.

While I'm spearing through the mountains, here's what's happening. Quattro drive normally ⁘

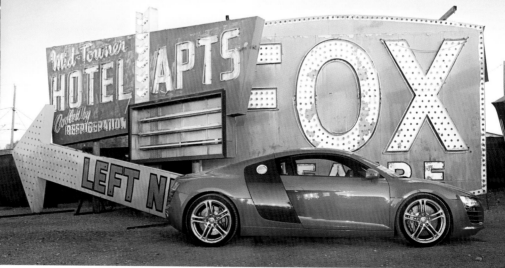

The devil's in the detail – like the R8 engraving in the headlights

Carbon fibre encased fuel filler cap – ultimate style

sends just 15 per cent of the effort forward, so the steering stays pretty pure. But when the rear tyres are losing it – either spinning under power or dragging under lift-off – the oversteer gets quelled by sharing torque forward, up to 35 per cent, which pulls you straight. The suspension is a long-travel design (and like the spaceframe, almost entirely different from a Gallardo's) so as to allow extra breathing room over big bumps. There's even an extra link in the rear double-wishbones to control toe angle (and hence lift-off oversteer) when the wheels are at the ends of their travel.

Gradually it becomes clear it's up for proper powerslides. The ESP has three stages: normal, low-threshold and off. I'm in the mid-setting and it's gloriously laissez-faire, allowing half-a-turn of opposite lock and a corresponding 180-degree grin. Later, on the track, I'm watching the guy who engineered it as he drifts into a second-gear corner on the brakes. By the way, he says you can actually spin it in the low-threshold mode, so I'd advise the normal mode in the wet.

Bottom line: handling is the core business of a mid-engined supercar, and this one, more than any other, flatters a normal driver (me), but allows you to get to know it and reward your skill.

At the track, I'm quite liking the optional £5,200 R tronic clutchless paddleshift. It shifts fast and your hands stay on the wheel. On the road, I hate it. It's not a DSG, but a flappy-paddle automated manual. It's jerky through town and thumps its upshifts at mid-effort acceleration. The manual has a slick, open-gated shift and a fairly light clutch, and is to be preferred over the R tronic as a nice Bordeaux is over a mug of cold sick.

Having so adored driving the R8, I'm bound to be skewed positively towards the design. Admittedly the bodyshell doesn't quite serve up the everyday supercar promised: it's too wide, it's tricky to see out of in some directions and there's a lot less boot than in a Cayman. But if you don't like the look of it, let its designer Frank Lamberty explain it. First, the aero is excellent for drag, stability, downforce and cooling. And it's not a pastiche of other supercars: the front is higher, the windscreen more upright than the Gallardo for instance, which is partly why the spaceframe is different, though built by similar methods.

The sideblades look added-on, but if you follow their surfacing and cut-lines you see they're the most integrated air intakes of any mid-engined car. They also help to visually shorten the R8,

which has a longer wheelbase than the Gallardo. I'd have a dark grey R8 with orange blades.

Deep breath. Time to stick my neck out. The R8 does it. Sure it isn't as visceral or edgy to drive as it might have been – more initial bite to the steering, brakes and throttle wouldn't hurt. But it's an easy thing to form a bond with because it's so open with you, and it won't irritate you. If you don't like Audis because they're smug and haughty, let this one turn you. And put the backlash on hold.

You can't see them here, but LED indicators are very cool

'The manual 'box has a slick, open-gated shift and a fairly light clutch, and is to be preferred over the R tronic as a Bordeaux is over a mug of cold sick'

Green Wing

The 911 GT3 may be the last flat-six RS Porsche ever makes, which means it could be a classic... even if Richard Hammond does hate that colour

Story by Richard Hammond
Photography by Joe Windsor-Williams

RK07 YGT

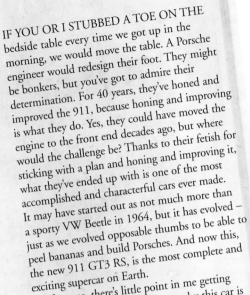

IF YOU OR I STUBBED A TOE ON THE bedside table every time we got up in the morning, we would move the table. A Porsche engineer would redesign their foot. They might be bonkers, but you've got to admire their determination. For 40 years, they've honed and improved the 911, because honing and improving is what they do. Yes, they could have moved the engine to the front end decades ago, but where would the challenge be? Thanks to their fetish for sticking with a plan and honing and improving it, what they've ended up with is one of the most accomplished and characterful cars ever made. It may have started out as not much more than a sporty VW Beetle in 1964, but it has evolved – just as we evolved opposable thumbs to be able to peel bananas and build Porsches. And now this, the new 911 GT3 RS, is the most complete and exciting supercar on Earth.

Of course, there's little point in me getting snared up in an argument about why this car is better than all the others, because supercars are ultimately a matter of individual taste, and you can't argue against that. James chooses to grow his hair long, because he thinks it looks good. No amount of arguing that he looks like a spaniel mated with a tramp will ever persuade him otherwise; it's a case of personal taste. Look at our 100 Fastest Cars list at topgear.com and you'll see what I mean – you're sure to disagree with some of it. But what I can do here is explain why, for me, this car is *the boss*, and maybe you'll be able to relate to at least some of what I'm on about.

You probably know about the GT3, Porsche's stripped-out version of the 911 designed for racing homologation. To make it, the normally aspirated 911 lost its rear seats (and other bits and pieces) to shed weight – it's 30kg lighter than a Carrera S – and gained a racing roll cage. To turn it into a GT3 RS, Porsche put it on a more extreme regime, with a different, more complex cage, lightweight carbon-fibre rear wing and Perspex rear window, saving another 20kg. About 700 will be produced, guaranteeing exclusivity. And that RS livery means a lot – some sensational cars have worn it in the past, like the 1972 2.7 RS. That's enough to make the £14k premium over the GT3 more than worth it, even forgetting the improved resale value. Oh, and it looks a bit meaner than the GT3, because it uses the slightly wider rear bodywork (it has a 44mm wider rear track, to be exact) from the Turbo and Carrera 4.

The 3.6-litre flat-six in the GT3 is a very different animal to the one in the standard 911, using a lot of parts from the racing GT1 motor – exhaust, headers, intakes and the ECU have all been fettled, and its special twin-cast blocks make the engine stiffer and capable of producing more power. The RS version is also fitted with a slightly lighter flywheel than the regular GT3 for even ⠶

easier revving. The figures are impressive – 415bhp at 7,600rpm and 299lb ft at 5,500rpm. That makes it the most powerful normally aspirated, six-cylinder engine in production, and in a car the size of a small hatchback, 415bhp is plenty. Standstill to 62mph takes 4.2 seconds – some magazines have got it as being below 4.0 – and you're doing 100mph in 10 seconds dead, on the way to a maximum of 187mph. Sheesh.

But figures are just figures, numbers on a page. It's the way the engine does its job that blows me away. You can potter off down the shops in it and it never bites – it's tractable and benign. But for God's sake, don't go shopping in it. Just because you can, doesn't always mean you should. Please, please beat this car mercilessly until you think it can take no more. Because it can and, on this occasion, you definitely should. It revs with a furious, charging energy – it thrives on revs, and it never, ever feels anything other than urgent when you want to push on.

One of the great things about this car is its purity of purpose. When a Ferrari is finished, it's sort of garnished with character, like ketchup on chips. Porsche doesn't do that. It finishes the car and then it is what it is. And that sense is nowhere better expressed than in the engine. It doesn't have a nice Perspex cover above it to say 'ooh, here I am and aren't I lovely?' It doesn't have pretty valve covers or badging or exposed exhaust manifolds. No. It's the ugliest engine in Christendom – it looks like the back of an old washing machine. And who gives a bugger? Because it doesn't need

to look any different – it's designed to slam the car down the road as fast as possible. And sod beauty, it's the driving that counts.

If it looks like a washing machine, then it certainly sounds like one. The lack of aesthetic buggering about extends to the engine sound – at least at low revs. It's all mashing, clattering valves and mechanical din invading the cabin. Sure, the Porsche guys could engineer a lot of that roughness out, they could acoustically tune it, but why? It's not a clarinet, it's a supercar engine. The noise it makes is a direct result of the purpose the engineers have set for it. If you love it – and many of us do – then great, the Porsche guys appreciate your understanding. If you hate it, they couldn't give a flying fig. Buy a CD of pretty V8 engine sounds and play it, if that's what you want. Play it in your BMW.

It's when you let it off the leash that its real character shouts at you – a howl that makes me grin like, well, like a bloke at the wheel of someone else's £94k Porsche supercar every time I hear it. This sound couldn't be anything other than a Porsche flat-six, but it's louder and more aggressive in this GT3 than the standard Carrera. It is simply a more extreme expression of the same beast in standard form.

I can't tell you how much I love a Porsche for its lack of pretence, its lack of engineered-on glitz and garnish. It doesn't need added character, because it has character oozing from every micron. And let's not forget, they may only be numbers on a page, but those figures also mean

it's stunningly fast in real life – that 10-second 0-100mph time is only 10ths away from a Turbo.

Here's a thing – why don't you see more Lamborghinis and Ferraris and Astons at the Nürburgring Nordschleife, the world's greatest, most demanding race track? Because they're not built to take it, and their owners aren't the sort of drivers who'd enjoy thrashing their expensive cars round there. They would rather admire the engine through its Perspex lid or listen to their CD of V8s singing opera. But go to the 'Ring a public day and the place is chock-full of 911 GT3s. That's purity of purpose for you.

Another spin-off of the Porsche obsession w fettling is a sense of continuity and lineage. If you put me in the passenger seat of any curre 911, blindfolded me and put ear muffs on m could still tell we were in a 911. It has a disti

'One of the great things about this car is its purity of purpose. When a Ferrari is finished, it's garnished with character. Porsche doesn't do that

Stereo? Pah, who needs a stereo, when you've got a flat-six to listen to?

"It'd just be our secret. All you need to say is that you lost it..."

the engine, it's the car's most impressive quality. Or is it the chassis? I can't decide. It's all good. Punt it through a high-speed bend and as you'd expect, the grip levels are gigantic – at least they are in the dry on these Michelin Sport Cup tyres. Streaming wet and slippery conditions might be a bit more hairy. Lift off, and you still get that 911 oversteer moment as the mass of the engine pivots beyond the rear axle, but it's under control – yours to use if you feel the need. And have the balls. And, of course, the stability control will let you slide it a bit before it catches the car. Or you can turn it off. This is a track-focused machine that any racing driver would be immediately at home in. I'm not a racing driver, not by any means, but I can certainly appreciate how direct and agile this car is. And if you love driving as much as I do, you'd love it too.

I was expecting the ride to be a lot harder than it is. Even when you hit the Sport button – which firms up the dampers – the ride is still comfortable and compliant. Porsche's active damper system had the purists howling when it was first released, but I think they've probably gone a bit quiet now. The compromise between ride and handling is pure magic. I drove this car hard for a good two hours on some pretty bumpy roads, and none of my teeth got broken. You never find yourself avoiding bumps to save your spine, and the body-hugging lightweight racing seats, though hard, seem to match the compliance of the ride perfectly.

bobbing motion at the front end that has been there since the Sixties. It's a function of the weight of the engine being where it is and the compliant but firm damping, and I love it. That's not to say it's unstable or in any way dangerous – this is the most planted car you can imagine. It's as if the nose is a bit restless, sniffing for another corner to attack. The steering chatters away in your hands, alive and full of feel. You sense every tiny bump on the road surface, every ridge and dip. OK, the downside is that it can tramline quite badly on occasion, but you can live with it, because the alternative is a numbness that just wouldn't be a Porsche 911. It is talking to you constantly through the suede rim, and the lightest thought of a movement in your hands will have the car changing direction. Along with

Anything I don't like? Well, the seat is set way too low for a bloke of my height, but that's easily sorted. And I'm not sure about the suede all over the place – I'm not a fan of Alcantara and if I could spec the car without it, I would. And, er, I'm struggling to think of much more. Other than the colour. It's too green. And the orange is too orange. I think I'd have the world's greatest performance car in black – a car can't be too black.

This could be the last of the flat-six 911s, so perhaps we should pause for thought. There are rumours flying around about Porsche working on a new flat-eight engine – that it has decided it has squeezed all it can out of six cylinders and it's time to move on. Once again, the purists will be jumping up and down in a worried frenzy about the death of the six, and I must admit, I feel a pang of anxiety when I think about this great engine being scrapped. Still, as the last flat-six 911 GT3 RS, the car you're looking at is probably a classic already.

But we mustn't get too worried about the future of the 911, because there's one thing you can bet your house on – that the eight will be better than the six, and that the next 911 GT3 RS will be better than this car. The ultimate 911 is always the latest 911 – quite an achievement. I find it impossible to imagine how they could improve it, but that's why I'm not a Porsche engineer. In fact, I'm pretty sure if you or I hung around at the factory gates at Weissach for long enough, we too would find ourselves improved. ■

'Lift off, and you still get that 911 oversteer moment as the mass of the engine pivots, but it's under control — yours to use if you feel the need'

Black Magic

It's called the CLK Black, and under the tough-looking skin it's a Ferrari-bothering supercar. **Jeremy Clarkson** wants one...

'This car's starting-point is an AMG CLK, which normally comes with a 474bhp, 6.2-litre V8. But for the Black, some fiddling has taken that past 500bhp'

I N MOTORING, IT GOES WITHOUT saying that certain things are mutually exclusive. You can't, for instance, have a low-slung sports car which works off road; you can't have a high top speed and good economy; and you can't have your dignity if you also have a small Korean hatchback.

Also, despite many claims to the contrary, you can't have a car which performs well on the Nürburgring and on the ring road. Or, at least, you couldn't until now...

You may imagine that the car you see in the pictures is some kind of DTM racer for the road, as hard as nails, as focussed as a laser and impossibly uncomfortable should you ever be asked to drive across, say, Keith Richards's face.

It isn't. What you're looking at here is the only car I know which really does achieve the impossible. A car that could quite happily get you, and more luggage than you could imagine, actually to Beijing. But which, I suspect, could quite happily bite chunks out of a Porsche turbo's arse on a twisting and deserted piece of Welsh A road.

It comes from the skunk works deep inside the special projects division Mercedes calls AMG. And it's badged simply, and in newsprint-sized letters, as the Black.

The first Black was a disaster. Merc fitted a hard carbon roof, along with hard carbon suspension

to an SLK and was undoubtedly very pleased with the way it could handle a race track. But the engineers were so nervous about the way it might feel in the real world, they wouldn't actually let me try one. "It's not very nice," said a Mercedes spokesman. And, from what I can gather from my colleagues who did have a go – many of whom are now being fed mashed food through a tube up their nose – they were right.

The new Black is different. The starting-point is an AMG CLK, which normally comes with a 474bhp, 6.2-litre V8. However, for the Black, a bit of fiddling with the exhaust and the electronics has taken that up past 500bhp. Never mind Porsche. We're deep in Ferrari territory here.

Inside, the posh seats have been replaced with body-hugging buckets. They're so body-hugging in fact, that I'd challenge even Jon Bon Jovi to get behind the wheel and do his seatbelt up.

Other things? Well the seat motors have gone, along with the satnav, the motor for the steering column adjustment, the back seats, and some of the airbags. In addition, the door panels are now carbon fibre, and the net result of all this is that the Black weighs just a tiny bit more than when the engineers started.

That's mainly because it has a Brunellian rear axle and a diff made from granite. Oh, and just about the best body kit I've ever seen. ⁛

For the Black, this little lump gets an upgrade to a massive 507bhp

Admittedly, some carbon fibre was harmed in the making of this interior

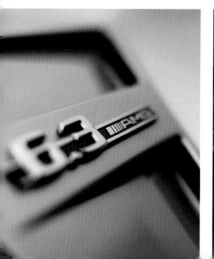

No back seats? Hell, no – back seats slow you down. But dig those buckets

Also good for field-hopping and a spot of gnarled tree action

Auto shifter looks innocent enough. But then so does Robert Mugabe

'I loved this car. I loved the speed. I loved the way it looked. And I loved the way it handled with a panache that would have Ferrari test drivers nodding sagely'

The net result is stunning. Initially, it scares you half to death because it seems to be dancing down the road, and then you realise it is dancing. You're just telling it where to go.

I loved this car. Adored it. I loved the noise when it started, a huge bellowing "hello". I loved the speed. I loved the way it looked. And I loved the way that when I took it to a Welsh mountain, it gripped and handled with a panache that would have the Ferrari test drivers nodding sagely. You really can talk about this thing in the same breath as a 430.

But here's the kicker. It's not a Ferrari. It's a Mercedes CLK. And yes, while some of the normal stuff has been binned, it still has an auto gearbox, plumbing for a phone, cruise and that Germanic integrity on a motorway. It even rides properly. I'd say it's smoother than my SLK55.

What's more, because the rear seats have gone – and the EU won't let you put them back in again, in case the moon goes out of orbit or some such nonsense – there is more space in the back than you get in most barns. It even has a system which allows you to play your iPod and see on the dash display what track you're hearing.

See what I mean? It's a normal car. But it goes like a rocket. And thanks to carbon-ceramic brakes, it stops pretty tidily as well. A Ferrari is awesome in the right place, but buggers its nose everywhere else, and the leather squeaks and the headlights are no good. The Black is brilliant, everywhere, at absolutely everything. By miles and miles, it's my new favourite car.

There is just one catch. Even though it comes with less stuff than a normal AMG CLK, it costs a ridiculous £34,000 more. Yes. You read that correctly. The Black is a six-figure car, and that's way too much.

It should cost £66,000 – the same as the standard car – so that buyers have a choice. A car that's kind to your hands. Or one that does the dishes as well.

Even so, I shall doff my cap to anyone who buys this thing. A Ferrari or a Porsche may well say more about you to more people. But a Black targets what it says to just a select few. And what it says, very quietly, is this: "If you really know your cars, you know why the person behind the wheel bought this..."

God, I want one. 🔲

Smokin

It had to happen. The age of the diesel supercar has dawned.
But should Ferrari and friends be worrying about Audi's R8 V12 TDI? Oh yes...

Words: Bill Thomas
Photography: Justin Leighton

I LET THOMAS KRÄUTER DRIVE FIRST. His surname is pronounced 'Kroyter', and he's one of the car industry's many unsung heroes – a backroom wizard creating masterworks of engineering and not getting much credit for it. There are hundreds like him, and they're happy to beaver away at the things they love, knowing they've got some of the best jobs imaginable. And what a job his is. He's the technical project leader on the Audi R8 V12 TDI Le Mans concept you see here, which – although this hasn't been confirmed officially – will soon become the greatest Audi road car of all.

"This is something new," says Thomas, as I motion him to take the driver's seat. He's been asked the same boring questions over and over by the stampede of journalists from all over the world who have decamped to Miami for a spin in this thing, so it was refreshing to do some driving instead.

I have other reasons for being happy riding shotgun. I don't want any distractions from the single aspect of this car I am most curious about – its sound. We're stepping into the unknown here, the first supercar of its kind. Much of it might seem 'normal'; it has a six-litre, 60-degree V12 mounted amidships, with two massive turbochargers fed by a big NACA duct on the roof. Excellent. It develops 500bhp and 738lb ft of torque, which is 86bhp and 421lb ft more than the standard V8 petrol R8. Decent. The engine, lifted straight from the V12 TDI Touareg, is an exceptional one. But this is a supercar, and it's a diesel. How must it *sound?*

Thomas punches the starter button, mounted Ferrari mannetino-like on the steering wheel, and there is a brief whirr and then a zimmy sound. Don't know how to describe it other than 'zimmy sound', like a giant, extremely powerful sewing machine.

It's coming from behind our heads, and though it's by no means as intrusive as most mid-engined supercars, you're in no doubt that something significant is lurking back there.

The zimmy sound is accompanied by heavy breathing from the induction system, a compressed, hollow whoosh. And in the dim distance, like a far-away moan of some giant owl, is a deeper whine, very subtle but unmistakably a big-engine note. Thomas's take on it is just as surreal as mine: "It's like 12 dwarves working, the cylinders, though they are not so small these dwarves." They certainly aren't. There isn't a hint of 'dieselness' or clatter, other than a very faint stuttering rhythm to the note at higher revs.

Thomas gives it no revs as we roll away on our brief journey down a quiet road near the harbour in Miami. Then he gives it more revs when he gets into third. Engine noise builds, but it's still a high-pitched mechanical zim dominating,

The future starts here. It'll be fun. And it'll sound like a giant owl

along with a monstrous pipe-hitting breathing from the turbos. The turbo whoosh dominates everything when you start to move along at pace. It's all turbo, this engine. It's a massive hollow pipe rush, like hearing white noise played at full blast down a two-foot-wide metal pipe.

Thomas grins. Then he says something. And when you read the next line, read it in a German accent because it works better. I'm not poking fun, I'm just remembering what he said and how he said it. And he's German, like a human embodiment of *Vorsprung durch Technic.* So, get that accent ready…

"Something strange is working behind us." Strange. And fantastic. I think I almost like it.

Now it's my turn to slot behind that beautiful flat-bottomed wheel. Thomas has turned the wick right down for our run here, so only half the torque is on tap. The A4 gearbox fitted to the concept is at fault. I know this because I asked Thomas to turn the wick right up, get his laptop out just for me, so that I could feel *The Torque.* I explained that I didn't need to drive it at full snap, but would be happy to feel it working at über-boost from the passenger seat.

"See that sign over there?" he answered, pointing to a road sign about 50 yards away. Yep. "The gearbox would be disintegrated entirely before we reached it."

A new gearbox design will be needed for this car, then, an investment I hope Audi decides to sign off. For now, we need to be gentle. I leave the engine ticking over, let the clutch out, and clack up through the R8's metal open-gate gearbox without touching the throttle pedal. There's probably 60 per cent of max torque available at the 600rpm tickover, so I use it, and am in top gear before I know it, doing about 21mph at 600rpm. At tickover. Astonishing torque, even at half-wick. Got to remember this ❧

As a diesel, you can expect a bit of low-end torque from the R8 TDI

'The zimmy sound is accompanied by a hollow whoosh. And in the dim distance, a deeper whine, an unmistakable, big-engine note'

Evil-eyed, but not quite the devil the petrol is with fuel costs

This roof duct keeps the turbos happy. Not to be used as storage

Great Audi build quality. But is that red stitching all a bit 1980s?

Honeycomb and slats form part of a design that still has its critics

Kept behind a glass case is a work of art sure to win admirers

Four-wheel drive means it grips better than most on the bends

At present, it's a gearbox from the A4. Not for long, though...

is only half of it: 738lb ft must be really something, because 370 feels grunty enough, though there's nothing much to be learned on this silly low-speed drive. Thomas says the gearing will go higher with the production car.

You need to recalibrate your head with this thing. I floor the throttle at 600rpm in sixth and it pulls smoothly and cleanly, with a deep bellow and a hardening of the engine note as the revs build v-e-r-y slowly. Drop two gears, and you have awesome acceleration on tap – apparently, it will pull away in fourth gear without drama. Later, when I am doing the 'driving photo', I let the thing run almost to the red line at full throttle – sorry Thomas – and by God, the thrust is alien at higher revs. It seems to come from nowhere as those turbos spool up effortlessly. That red line happens at a low 4,500rpm, at which speed a Ferrari engine would only just be coming on cam.

Recalibrate your brain, BT. What would this thing be like to live with? Effing incredible, is the answer. The engine is only 89kg heavier than the R8's petrol V8, and it's mounted further forward, which helps the handling. Serious drivers haven't driven it yet, but Thomas says they will like it, says it's a real bruiser on the track, with no discernible difference in balance to the petrol car. I believe him.

The big unit feels light and revvy. There is almost no flywheel effect – this is a blippy, sporty, light-feeling engine. Thomas says the flywheel had to be small, given the space restriction of the layout. Precise heel-and-toe driving on a track would be a doddle.

The real wonder of this car will be its breadth of abilities. Unbelievable flexibility and effortless acceleration at all speeds with its monstrous torque output. Relatively good fuel-efficiency and quiet long-distance cruising, with the knowledge of the torque being there when you need it. So that'll make it a proper GT. And, last but not least, four-wheel-drive quattro grip in bad weather, combined with a nimble, light-footed, mid-engined feel on twistier stuff – direct, sharp steering, clamped-to-the-road grip, easy oversteer on demand, supercar fun. Oh, and carbon-ceramic brakes to rein in all that speed. The car will do 186mph, passing 62mph in only 4.2 seconds and 100mph in about 10 seconds. And it'll return up to 29mpg in normal driving.

The bigger picture is interesting. Why does this car exist? To be the ultimate Audi, probably

– one that will be more expensive and more exclusive than any other R8, and built in smaller numbers. Given that the normally aspirated V10 from the S6 and Audi-owned Lamborghini Gallardo will soon be used to create the new RS8, probably running at around 480bhp and 430lb ft, this mighty diesel powerplant neatly takes the car in a new direction. Importantly, it provides Audi a cool, high-tech marketing tool to attract those all-important US customers to the brand and, crucially, to a new type of fuel. Diesel hasn't caught on in the States yet – but as fuel prices rise, no doubt it will. Audi will be right there, with a range of efficient, economical Bluetech diesels that will fly off the forecourts with a little help from this monster, linked as it is to the R10 racer hissing around the American Le Mans series and winning everything in sight. Or not winning, as the case may be.

Expect the TDI to be differentiated from 'normal' R8s in all sorts of ways other than its engine. Big duct on the roof, big engine ducting visible through the rear glass, different nose and tail and skirts like this concept, which has more intake area up front and different mesh, maybe different wheels and cabin. The ultimate Audi.

We'll have to wait for a drive in the production car to be sure, but I suspect Audi has created something special here. The diesel supercar has arrived, and it'll worry those old-school, high-revving, inefficient, noisy supercars out there.

"Something strange is working behind us." You're not wrong, Thomas. But it's something extraordinary, too. [TG]

'What would this thing be like to live with? Effing incredible is the answer. It feels light and revvy. Precise heel-and-toe driving on a track would be a doddle'

Bill about to emerge from R8 in lemon espadrilles and pink suit

The Bug Club

Is this what they mean by an oasis in the desert, three Veyrons blasting down their own private highway? **Bill Thomas** rubs his eyes in disbelief

Photography by Lee Brimble

'In an almost unprecedented act of generosity, we ended up with three 1,000,000-euro Veyrons. That's two more than we actually needed'

If only the promenade at Southend-on-Sea was this beautiful

Pur Sang Veyron spotted through red Veyron with white Veyron

Strangely quiet on this road... because the cops shut it just for us

FOR A FEW MOMENTS, WE could have been in a one-make Veyron race on the streets of Abu Dhabi, blasting down the Corniche road, the magnificent coastal city stretch with the bright blue waters of the Gulf and a golden beach on one side, and spectacular high-rise buildings on the other, and there was no speed limit because the police had closed it for us. Nice. We'd rounded a bend, and not one but two Veyrons slid left to right into place in my Veyron's rear-view mirror, red and chrome, one behind the other, snick snick, both dropping back briefly as I nailed the throttle

an instant before they did, then running up to 150mph in a blink, three of the greatest supercars the world has ever seen, together in one of the most sleek and modern cities in the world. With the blessing of the cops. Driving doesn't get a hell of a lot better than this.

Three Veyrons. And one of them is a chrome Pur Sang special edition, one of only five in the world. Beyond motor shows, no one's seen one of these before. It could only happen in Abu Dhabi, the richest of the United Arab Emirates, and it happened almost by accident.

We had a Koenigsegg flown in from Sweden, but the Veyron we'd organised to meet it in battle had dropped out at the last minute. So the call went out, and it went right to the top. We'll talk about that a bit later, but, in an almost unprecedented act of generosity, we ended up with three 1,000,000-euro Veyrons. Two more than we needed. And three's most definitely better than one when it's Veyrons.

And then the Koenigsegg wouldn't start. Seriously. A silly little problem with a fuel line meant it was sucking down vapour, coughing :·

Handling mode on the Bugatti means rear spoiler / brake fully extended

The Pur Sang. An exterior that lets its driver bask in all that reflected glory

and spluttering, as the police closed down the roads and the helicopter cameras spooled up, ready for the shoot. Aargh. The plan was to shoot the four cars together, but this meant we had to do the Koenigsegg versus the Veyron the next day in the mountains, and just concentrate on these three for the city shoot. It didn't matter much.

Three great stretches of road were closed for us in succession in the early hours of a Friday morning, the equivalent of a Sunday in the Arab world and the quietest time of the week. This was great. The welcome for *Top Gear* from Abu Dhabi was

truly overwhelming – for them to go to all this trouble just shows you what these guys are all about. Friendship, hospitality and cars. And they're dead serious about their car culture here. Look at the rear wing of an F1 Ferrari, and you'll see Etihad Airways written across it, national carrier for the UAE and the guys who flew our Koenigsegg. Look at the flanks of a works Ford World Rally Car and you'll see Abu Dhabi there, in bold. This is a city and a country which will soon be very much on the international stage, and cars and motorsport figure large in their plans – the first Abu Dhabi

Grand Prix won't do any harm, either. It's very likely we'll be back here, doing something even bigger and better. Watch this space.

Back to the shoot. First, a long stretch of 30th street (Khaleej Al-Arabi) was closed. Here we ran to about 150mph in convoy, the cars utterly stable and solid at this speed, the equivalent of doing 70mph in a family hatch, a giggle. Then the Corniche road was made available to us, which included a couple of nice long sweepers that the Veyrons hardly noticed. But, boy, it felt good slamming the car through them, feeling the

'For them to go to all this trouble just shows you what these guys are all about. Friendship, hospitality and cars'

Why have one when you can have three? Our Veyrons wait patiently

Count 'em: 48 cylinders, 2,961 horsepower, six airscoops and over £2m

the g pile on as the 'handling mode' rear wing bit into the air. Then we ran down the breakwater, which runs out into the Gulf at right angles to the Corniche, and links the main part of the city with Marina Village. Check it out on Google Maps – it's a cool place. As a part of our plan to shoot Veyron v Koenigsegg, it would have been tremendous – but with three Veyrons, it was somehow even better.

As the cars were loaded back onto their trucks, it occurred to me that allowing a few strangers to

have a go in my £850K supercar might not come too easy to me. Luckily, these guys are obviously much more generous than I'll ever be.

They're also proper petrolheads that we can safely say – as Top Gear fans – that you'd get along just fine with.

The first, who owns the Pur Sang, is a member of the royal family, and an all-round good guy. The other two Veyrons belong to Sheikh Hazza Bin Tahnoon Al Nahyan. Yes *the other two* – the white and red ones. They're into cars!

Thanks to their generosity, *Top Gear* has

been able to write possibly the best feature in the world, ever. With the best cars in the world, ever. It's all worked out beautifully. Amazing. And, no, I'm not overstating the case – where else have you seen a feature like this? Nowhere, that's where. This is a world first – three Veyrons, one chrome.

A full and heartfelt *Top Gear* shout must therefore go to these two car-loving sheikhs for making it possible, and no mistake. Yes, it's very likely we'll be back. Very likely indeed.

'It occurred to me that allowing a few strangers to have a go in my £850,000 supercar might not come too easy to me'

SOMETHING WICKED THIS WAY COMES

The most powerful AMG Mercedes ever, the SL65 Black, hits London's mean streets

Words: Sam Philip Photography: John Wycherley

A S THE BLACK ROLLS OFF THE ramps and into London's early evening gloom, the countdown begins. One single night. For all our begging and cajoling, that's all the time Mercedes has given us in the Black. Oh, and if it leaves London, moustachioed German heavies will turn up at *Top Gear* HQ and murder us in new and interesting ways. The most powerful AMG Merc ever, the SL65 Black, the car christened 'Der Beast' by its Frankenstein-esque creators, and we're limited to one night in the most congested, cramped city in Europe.

Just to make things interesting, the previous day has seen the heaviest snowfalls in Britain in 20 years. Snow that's freezing rapidly to sheet ice on the roads, making 670bhp and rear-wheel drive look a tad suicidal. Still, one night. The clock is ticking. Let's head underground.

The Blackwall Tunnel seems a good place to start. We spear south under the Thames, a thousand rings of dim, flaxy streetlight whipping backwards over the Black's flanks as it dives deeper below London. There is noise, and that noise is... whistling. The car is whistling. It's an ominous, unearthly noise, a murderous chorus of Roger Whittakers rising and falling as the turbos suck frozen air through the tunnel's south entrance and spit it out behind.

As the lights on the rev counter flash, climb and glow to red, the Roger Whittaker medley subsides. Now there's raw mechanical noise, a dozen cylinders threshing a metallic, overdriven chorus. Speed, too. The increments on the speedo are ticking off with alarming haste as the Black barrels out of the tunnel and back into the London night.

"That," says Dave, "is a proper tool." It's a compliment, we think. The Black is loitering under the railway arches in Rotherhithe, crackling and coughing as the frost – and local pigeon population – descends on south London. It's kicking-out time in the pub round the corner, and the Black is drawing a crowd. Dave's a proper East End geezer. You couldn't make him up. Knows his cars – used to 'borrow' 911s from the West End, but decided enough was enough after pulling a handbrake turn on the Old Kent Road with a dozen police cars in tow, he says. Dave approves of the Black. "Wider than my missus, that is," he says, tapping the giant, DTM-style arches. "Pity she don't go so quick." Not a bastion of political correctness, Dave.

He's right though. The Black is wide. Literally, figuratively. The longer you look at it, the more it seems to swell, to flex its anabolically enhanced flanks. Cast your eyes down from the roof: the top half of the Black's silhouette is stock SL – petite, proportioned, sensible, albeit with a carbon-fibre fixed roof (complete with integral roll cage) replacing the stock folding hard-top – but hit the top of the arches and it all goes steroidal. ⁘

Carbon-fibre spoiler raises 12cm at 75mph. Um, so we're told...

'The increments on the speedo are ticking off with alarming haste as the Black barrels out of the tunnel'

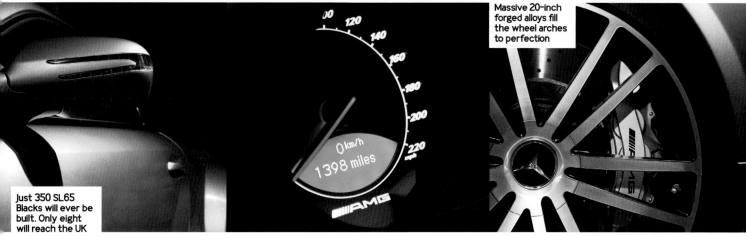

Just 350 SL65 Blacks will ever be built. Only eight will reach the UK

Massive 20-inch forged alloys fill the wheel arches to perfection

'There's enough give in the stability control for plenty of organ-rearranging moments of terror before the electronics kick in'

Carbon-fibre, start button, huge engine – Dr Frankenblack's been at work here

There's a full handspan of flare on either side, the stance of a gym-obsessed bulldog in Eighties shoulder-pads.

There's function behind the hulking form. The Black's engineers managed to shave 250kg – the equivalent of a pair of sturdy South London publicans – off the SL65's kerbweight, seemingly by employing the simple mantra, 'But what if we made it out of carbon fibre instead?' – the door panels, splitter, diffuser and most of the interior are rendered in black weave. The seats wouldn't be out of place in the Design Museum just up the road from here: gorgeous, sculpted carbon-fibre buckets, barely an inch thick. No tilt or lumbar adjustability here: you'll sit where you're told and be happy with your lot.

The SL65's mighty 6.0-litre V12 didn't escape Dr Frankenblack's knife, either. A pair of massive new turbos, larger air intakes and exhausts boost power from 612bhp to 670bhp – a full 53bhp more than the McMerc SLR, 69bhp more than the Ferrari 599. There's 737lb ft of torque available (or a pleasingly round 1000Nm in metric-speak), curbed by 20 per cent or so to prevent the SL's five-speed auto gearbox turning itself into a messy, cog-strewn interpretation of a cheese twist. On a warm, balmy day on, say, a race circuit in the south of France – Merc expects the Black to spend half its life on the track – this would be a wonderful thing to have under the deployment of your right foot. Right now, it's like having your toe trapped in the pin of a grenade.

Back into the night, and the pin is out. The Black's rear left wheel catches on a smattering of snow and launches into a lairy, lurid slide across the London night. Jeez. Ease off. Easy. We're out of the tunnels now, cranking up the big V12 across East London's industrial wasteland. It's the sort of area described by property developers as 'ripe for regeneration' and by *Top Gear* as 'a bad place to crash a hyper-exclusive supercar'. Or run out of fuel. The economy readout flashes 7.8mpg as the tyres scrabble and scrape for grip on the ice-basted roads. This much is clear: on frozen, snow-strewn tarmac, the Black is a nasty little bastard that you don't want to cross. It's a car that exists in a realm of grip several continents away from where we are at the moment, a sunny land of wide, sticky roads and gentle, soft verges.

Still, one night. One icy, deserted night. Go again. Christ, this thing is quick. Even in these skating-rink

conditions, Merc's claim of a sub-four second 0-60mph time feels eminently believable. Top speed of 199mph? We'll trust you on that one, guys.

Traction control is on. Fully on. Even so, there's enough give in the stability control to allow for plenty of organ-rearranging moments of terror before the electronics kick in to tidy things up. Slide, catch, slide, catch. Wipe palms on jeans. Make weak, terrified joke. Concentrate. An unintended extra millimetre or two of squeeze on the accelerator sends the Black lurching merrily towards a snow bank. With frozen feet and a frozen brain, this is not good news. Time to slow down.

Even at crawling speed, the Black is a visceral experience. Every shard of grit, dumped just hours before, clacks and pings against the undertray, every patch of lumpy snow crunches audibly under the tyres. Manoeuvring on full lock between the desolate warehouses, the diff clunks and heaves, the roof creaks alarmingly. There's almost zero suspension travel, so the entire car hops and skips over dents and divots.

Still, the Black remains a confusing car. Tough to shake the sensation that it doesn't quite know what it wants to be. Elements of it are as focussed and hardcore as they come: the rock-hard springs, the lethal brakes, the sheer stiffness of the thing. But the five-speed auto – even in maximum-attack manual mode – feels numb and slow-witted in comparison. Difficult to know when you'd use the Black: it's just too noisy, too damn uncomfortable for a loping cross-continent schlep, but too unwieldy, too missile-like for the track.

Rarity alone will ensure the Black's desirability. Just 350 will ever be built, making even the 500-strong Ferrari Enzo look commonplace. Only eight will reach the UK, at a price of £250,000: a frankly insane amount of money, especially when you factor in the cost of employing your own personal weatherman to alert you to the three days a year when it's safe to actually use it.

And yet, and yet. For all its too-muchness, for all its bloody-minded, uncompromising bastardishness, there's something magical in the Black. Maybe it shares something with the snow that glints around us in the morning light: uncomfortable, slippery, downright dangerous in parts, but fascinating. You wouldn't want it every day, but you won't forget that one night. ▣

SL Black interior is mainly black - not too many surprises there

8 ON 10

The new Audi R8 has found another two cylinders and lost nothing in the process

Words: Paul Horrell Photography: Lee Brimble

G

OSH, AUDI HASN'T published a Nürburgring time for the R8 V10. Oh, the shame of it: the chat-room geeks will instantly conclude it's slower around that track in the hands of a driving god than a 911 Turbo or a Skyline. Having installed a 525bhp V10, is Audi now hanging its head in the disgrace of not ducking under the required number of minutes and seconds? Excuse me, I think you've confused me with someone who gives a stuff.

Can we just park, please, the sports-car world's increasing obsession with taking a stopwatch around the so-called 'legendary Nordschleife'? As you'll have deduced from the presence of number plates, this is a road car. What matters when you're on the road isn't the last few tenths. It's the feeling. The joy of working with a car, trusting it through an unknown corner, sensing its moves and its forces. Yes, speed and grip and braking power do matter, because in general terms the greater they are, the higher the potential exhilaration. But to gain a few fractions of cornering speed in exchange for losing some of the sensitivity is a very bad bargain indeed.

Audi knows this. The R8, in existing V8 form, is simply a sublime road car, unquestionably the one I'd have if the choice ran to the usual Carrera/GT-R/Vantage/Corvette suspects. That's because it is on your side. It's designed for ordinary drivers like me, not taciturn men in Nomex. It is easy to drive quickly, signalling its high limits clearly and then behaving with grace once it gets to them. And because of the 4WD, you can have more fun more of the time – it doesn't demand perfect weather.

So I am apprehensive about the £99,575 V10 version. Do two more cylinders mean a more cumbersome and less manageable drive? Do bigger tyres rob the delicacy? Has Audi fallen victim to the German horsepower race, chasing ever-higher numbers and disregarding the human factors? The R8 is my favourite pudding, and I don't want them over-egging it.

The engine is basically the one out of the Lamborghini Gallardo LP560-4, a £40,000 more expensive car. All that's different are the inlets and exhausts. The idea was to take away some of the noise, so that you can live with this car every day. Starting up a Gallardo in the morning will wake up your neighbours, and your neighbours' neighbours. The Audi's social acceptability costs 35bhp, knocking it back to 525. Just six per cent – nothing to worry about. Not when you can still squirt to 62 in 3.9secs, and keep going till you can see the whites of 200mph's eyes. It's a marvellous piece of engineering, using direct injection to resolve all sorts of apparent conflicts. Just think – more than 5.2 litres, yet it revs to 8,700, runs cleanly and has perfectly sweet traffic manners.

Those manners can be misleading. The power delivery is so miraculously even-handed that at first I was – can I say this without sounding absurdly blasé? – not entirely overwhelmed. For a start, faster cars do exist – the throttle isn't an instantaneous hyperdrive-switch, like it is in a ZR1 or Murciélago or Pagani. But more than that, because the R8 V10's output has no valleys, the peaks don't seem so high. There's strong pull from right down in the rev range, and that pull just gets stronger. And stronger. And stronger, until you do realise this is a proper supercar. And then stronger again, because you were shifting up at 6,000 and there's another 2,700 still to go...

But Audi wanted it to be civilised. And so, even as it's performing this wild and crazy stuff, ⁝

Do yourself a favour and don't spec the £5,090 automatic 'box

'The R8 is on your side. It's designed for ordinary drivers like me, not taciturn men in Nomex. It's easy to drive quickly'

Ha! Your day-time running lights aren't so exclusive now, are they R8?

Very Audi interior, only more so. And that can only be a good thing

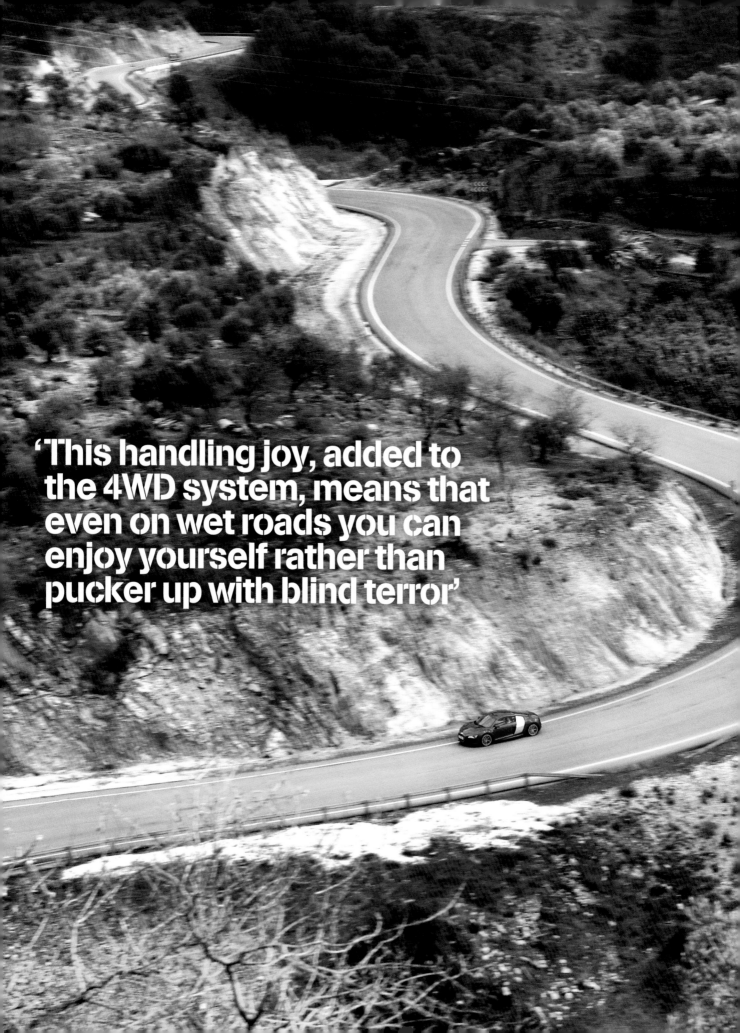

'This handling joy, added to the 4WD system, means that even on wet roads you can enjoy yourself rather than pucker up with blind terror'

Like the Pope, the V10 demands large windows in order to see its public

Don't panic. Those two extra cylinders only add to the joy you can have here

it sounds muted. It ought to sound like a V10 F1 car heard from the grandstands. Instead it sounds like a V10 F1 on a Playstation. Couldn't Audi have loosened the R8's necktie and allowed it to yell just a *little*? I mean, just at say 6,000-plus? It's not like that would have *so* ruined its peaceful mission.

We've got the optional R-Tronic on the test car. Pass notes in Audi jargon: R-Tronic is a paddleshift where the mechanism works the single clutch for you: the equivalent of Ferrari's F1. S-Tronic is Audi's double-clutch system. S-Tronic is good, R-Tronic isn't, not especially so. Nowhere near as good as the latest Ferrari F1 anyway, which manages to be both faster in the shifts and smoother all at the same time. Never mind, I love the manual option on the R8 – there's a metal gate so when you move the lever in just the right direction it slips home so gorgeously quickly and sharply. And it passes my personal criterion for a gearbox that really connects you to the cogs: you can actually feel the shift quality change as the oil warms up from cold. There, in recommending the manual, *TG* just saved you £5k.

The everywhereness and allthetimeness of the new engine's available power means the whole business of going around corners turns into a big-ticket stadium-scale event. Given that I so love the pub-gig intimacy of the R8 V8, I start to drive the V10 fretting that its bigger tyres, extra grip and harder suspension settings are going to take away the blissful sense of connection and balance that's really the R8's shining achievement.

Needn't have worried. It's as good as ever. What matters on the road is confidence, no matter your level of skill and experience. My skills are somewhere north of the 'average', so I am going to take every

crumb of it I can find. Confidence in the R8 comes three ways. First, the car tells you what it's up to, so find the limit. Second, when it does edge into slither mode, it's generally nicely balanced between front and back. And third, at that point it reacts predictably to your inputs. In fast corners, it stays level and immensely well-glued. Arriving at a slow bend, the throttle is the key. Things incline to mild oversteer if you give it the beans half-way round, but the steering is so helpful you're nudged into a simple correction. It's a magical feeling.

The combination of all this handling joy with the 4WD system and a well-calibrated set of electronics (with three switchable levels of intervention) means that even when the roads are greasy, you can enjoy yourself rather than puckering up with blind terror, parking and retiring for a nice restorative drink.

Most people with six-figure supercars probably have a few other vehicles to get themselves about. Well, with the R8, that's not necessary – and not just because it's OK in bad weather. It's also comfortable and perfectly practical, unless you need to carry kids (put them on the bus) or go through width-restrictors. There, in recommending you sell the 3-Series, *TG* just saved you another 20 grand.

It's not just that the R8 is quiet. It rides amazingly well, especially because superb magnetic-fluid adaptive dampers are standard. The cabin's fully kitted out, and don't bore me with this nonsense about how it's just like a big TT in here. It's not. There's a whole three-dimensional design theme to it that the TT lacks. And besides, the TT has one of the nicest cockpits in the business.

So there you have it – it *is* possible to improve on perfection. Just not by much.

Great Britain

British ingenuity and ideas have influenced sports car engineering for a century. Though the domestic car industry was torn apart in the 70s and 80s, small, very clever and hard-working companies remain.

Aston Martin has only recently been dethroned by iPhone as the coolest brand in the world. The association with James Bond – and more importantly the rich beauty and solidity of its cars – puts it 13 places above Ferrari. And 17 places above Rolex.

Then there are tiny, brilliant firms like Caterham, which will never see a coolbrands list, producing cars that are arguably even more of a phenomenon.

Stirling work

The most legendary living racing driver now has a car that bears his name – meet the awesome Mercedes McLaren SLR Stirling Moss

Words: Jason Barlow
Photography: Ripley & Ripley

Button on the right is the airbrake. Deploys at 85mph

Quilted seats are comfortable and help with any seepage

No radio – simply tune in to a 54-litre 650bhp engine instead

Double five-spokers on the Moss SLR look the business

COUPES, CONVERTIBLES, ROADSTERS, HIGHLY evolved Snetterton-spec special editions with Plexiglas windows: the car business is truly expert at charging more for less. This, though, surely takes the carbon-fibre biscuit.

The Mercedes McLaren SLR Stirling Moss costs 750,000 euro – £654,462, according to today's wildly fluctuating exchange rate – for which you don't even get a pair of windscreen wipers or a stereo system, not to mention the small matter of a missing roof. Obviously, it's also completely magnificent.

But what exactly is it? Well, amongst other things, the SLR Stirling Moss puts a full-stop on the McMerc road car collaborative story. Following 2003's original, the 722 limited-edition special and 2007's Roadster, this is the end of the road for a project that has happily – some would say recklessly – plundered the past and specifically the single greatest racing car of all time for inspiration. Sir Stirling Moss's epic and epochal Mille Miglia victory in the original 300 SLR is probably beyond even the slightest comparison with a modern car. But at least this run-out edition of the current SLR is sufficiently extreme not to despoil his name or what he achieved that famous day in May, 54 years ago.

Has the SLR really done the business for Mercedes-Benz and McLaren? As rumours about a deal between Merc and Aston Martin refuse to go away, and McLaren finishes its all-new mid-engined road car, you'd have to say things haven't panned out as harmoniously as expected. On the other hand, 1,500 SLR coupes and 500 Roadsters have been sold since the car's launch in November 2003, making it comfortably the biggest selling of all the Noughties' pre-recession hyper-cars, if not the most loved.

For some – owners mainly – the SLR's golf-club swallowing boot and intergalactic cruising potential made it the ultimate GT (I know of one car that racked up ⁑

'The SLR Coupe's cabin was hardly over-burdened, but this is something else: there's aircon, a gear lever, two seats and that's it'

19,000 miles in a year, something only a madman would consider in an Enzo or Carrera GT). For others – most of us in the office – its compromised philosophy left the SLR feeling unresolved. In fact, I've just re-read the conclusion to my first drive of the 722 version, back in the May 2007 issue of *Top Gear*: "We want an SLR Club Sport."

Well here it is, and then some. It's difficult to know where to start with this thing, but sitting in the driver's seat is as good a place as any. Only a contemporary Formula One car offers a view ahead as extreme as this; if anything, the scope and flow of the Merc's bonnet as it plunges out of the driver's line of sight in the distance means it's more extreme even than that. It certainly marks it out as possibly the most dramatic road car cockpit of all time. It feels like a giant – and rather more expensive – Caterham R500.

It's just as minimalist, too. The SLR Coupe's cabin was hardly over-burdened with toys, but this is something else: there's air-conditioning (primarily used for heating purposes, one can only assume) blowing through a pair of outsized air vents, a gearlever, two seats and that's about it. Even the gearlever itself has been minimised, wrongly in my view; the SLR's coolest interior party trick was the start button that lived under the grooved flip-top thing on the chunky gearlever, replaced here with a simpler leathery artefact.

The Stirling Moss's party trick is that there is no party trick, unless you count the mammoth sills. They're a full four inches higher than the already hefty items on the existing SLR, which, you may recall, once gave Britney Spears a spot of trouble...

There's more exposed carbon fibre on the enormous transmission tunnel than before, and the steering wheel is part-Alcantara covered. Like its 1950s progenitor, the SLR Stirling Moss also has dramatic-looking air scoops that double as roll hoops, giving the car's rear end a particularly fast-looking profile. ⋗

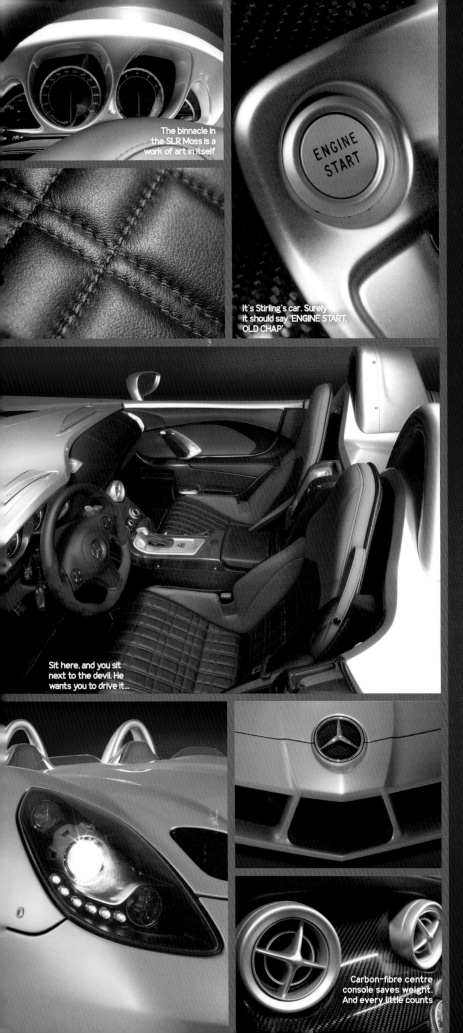

The binnacle in the SLR Moss is a work of art in itself

It's Stirling's car. Surely it should say 'ENGINE START, OLD CHAP'

Sit here, and you sit next to the devil. He wants you to drive it...

Carbon-fibre centre console saves weight. And every little counts

Better than all that, though, is the way the scuttle sweeps across to meet the interior; because there's no windscreen, you're much more aware of this bit of real estate than you'd normally be. The presence of those two tiny wind deflectors does little to alter this impression (if they were any higher than 36mm, legislation would have required them to have wipers). In fact, the panel actually swoops down to enclose the instruments, giving rise to the idea that the exterior bodywork is actually trying to *eat* the interior. Rarely have I sat in something that's so demonically tempting to drive.

Which would clearly have been a mistake, not least because the SLR Stirling Moss pictured here is the show car, and as such is limited to 10mph. Mind you, it's a proper runner, with the 722 edition-spec, 650bhp 5.4-litre supercharged engine tucked under that colossal bonnet, as it'll appear when production of the real thing begins (the suspension geometry is per 722, too). So while we wouldn't have got very far, we wouldn't have got very far very, very quickly indeed.

In fact, for a show car this really is an immaculately put together thing. What's more surprising is that it actually began life as a decommissioned SLR Coupe, which a small squad of McLaren's elite engineers set about with no doubt the finest tools money can buy. Apparently part of the product plan for well over a year, the call to preview the SLR Stirling Moss with a show car came so late in the day that it was touch and go. In the event, the car was done in about three months, with CAD used to model and verify the dimensions of the various new parts needed.

There were two main targets: to strip out at least 200kg from the Coupe's kerb weight, and to create something that would achieve a 350kph (217mph) top speed. Losing the roof and A-pillars is clearly key to this weight reduction, especially when the standard SLR's pillars contain a steel tube with a 6mm bore, to maximise roll-over protection and torsional rigidity. Despite these modifications, the SLR Stirling Moss apparently has the same stiffness as the Roadster, thanks to a cross-beam beneath the roll hoops. Besides, anyone who's ever seen a naked SLR tub will confirm that a lack of structural rigidity is not one of its issues.

Every single panel on the car is new – they're all fashioned out of carbon fibre, and in the flesh it's a convincing, though curvier and more Italian-looking, homage to Rudolf Uhlenhaut's original. There's a new side-exit exhaust system, and though the duct at the front of the bonnet mimics the equivalent detail on the Fifties SLR, it also helps cool the alternator underneath. At the rear, the SLR Coupe's stubby tail is now much slinkier and almost Aston DB9-like in detail. A vast rear diffuser is a vivid reminder that this car positively throbs with race-car DNA. Like all SLRs, the underbody is fully enclosed, and the airbrake carries over as a further aid to braking and overall stability.

If a more exhilarating road car emerges in 2009, then I'm not sure I'm quite ready for it. Whatever confusion may or may not have surrounded the SLR these past six years is blown to smithereens by the Stirling Moss iteration. Sharper, stiffer and lighter than a vehicle that was never short of dynamic drama in the first place, this isn't so much a car as a horizontal skydiving device.

'The car pictured here is a proper runner,
with a 650bhp 5.4-litre supercharged
engine tucked under that colossal bonnet'

GOLDFINGER
REMASTERED

After Clarkson and 007, the only bloke we know cool enough to own an Aston DB5 or consider its successor, the DBS, is Jon Claydon. So we asked him to compare them

Story by Jon Claydon Photography by Jason Furnari

ASTON MARTIN HAS, ONCE AGAIN, topped a poll of the world's coolest brands. That's not only car brands, mind. That's any brand at all. Whilst Apple, Prada and Sony battle for the minor places, a Warwickshire car factory (formerly, a shed in Newport Pagnell) bang out the hottest and most aspirational goodies in the rich man's playground. It's actually a little bizarre when you think about it.

For even more compelling evidence peruse the *TG* Cool Wall at your leisure. You, like I, had probably assumed that this was simply the impulsive and highly subjective judgement of the presenters, but the producer, Wilman – Yoda to Clarkson's Chewbacca – maintains otherwise. Candidate cars are apparently subjected to a complex algorithm by a small army of very clever men with hygiene issues employed solely, at the licence fee payers' expense, to evaluate their rightful spot on the Wall. And they put loads of Astons in the refrigerator section too.

Walk up to an Aston in the metal and you'll understand precisely why. Sexy? Trust me, drive any one of them and you'll feel like Englebert Humperdink in the showers of a 1968 nunnery. 007 invariably gets the credit for all this but there's more to Aston Martin than Pussy Galore. I have a DB5 and can personally vouch for the strange effect it has on people – drive one through London's notoriously hard to impress W11 and you'll feel like a wartime American soldier liberating an Italian village. That Sixties charisma would be hard to reproduce. How would its 2007 descendant measure up? Intriguingly, the DBS costs about the same as a decently restored DB5. Should I swap? Would you? Keeler or Keira? Connery or Craig?

Part of the charm of Sixties sports cars is that when parked next to their modern equivalents they look as if they belong to some long lost race of 4ft 6in humans. The DB5 is narrower than a Clio and parked next to the DBS it looked like Harry Potter chatting to Hagrid. What unites them is that they are both knockouts, and here we uncover the very simple and obvious secret of Astons' appeal. They're gorgeous. And producing a stunning GT these days – even for six figure sums – clearly isn't as easy as we thought. The Bentley Continental, by comparison, looks like an early Nineties MG with water retention issues;

A glamorous, if over-designed interior. As for the gearstick...

DB5 ranks as a heart-breaker from every angle

'When parked next to the DBS, the DB5 looked like Harry Potter chatting to Hagrid. But what unites them is that they are both absolute knockouts'

the strangely distended Ferrari 612 resembles a 599 bendy bus; and 911 Turbos and GT2s are a riot of spoilers and swollen arches. F430s and Modenas? Boys' cars, usually piloted by men who drive as if they're ejaculating. Only Bugatti looked a racing certainty to join Aston in the undisputed automotive Hall of Cool, but it hasn't. Yes, the Veyron is a technological masterpiece, and with 1,000 horsepower it's probably the first car in which you can break the national speed limit while parking. But it costs £900,000, and if you apply a normal supercar depreciation rate (they lose about a third of their value after the first 20,000 miles) your Sunday lunchtime spin from, say, a nobby SW1 mews to a Cotswolds' pub and back will cost you, all in, about £3,500. And I don't care how much money you have, that's not cool.

All of which leaves Aston in a pretty much unassailable position, at least as far as women are concerned. The Great Unspoken Truth about Aston's brand is that, as Batman put it, chicks dig the car, and the DBS has quite enough charisma to carry the torch. Having said that, the female passer-by response to it was rather different to what I'm used to with

the DB5. Such is the presence of the thing that it triggered what I call the reverse rubber-neck syndrome, where in their determination not to look at you, people turn their heads 90 degrees in the opposite direction and, occasionally, hurtle into lamp posts. Is it an appropriate successor to the iconic DB5? Absolutely, though the regular DB9 fills that role more directly. There may have been about 114 different owners of the company between these two models, but the DNA is perfectly recognisable. First of all, and as with the DB5 before it, it's not quite as good as it looks. Pale men wearing cardigans who don't get out enough will insist on telling you that there are £60k German saloons that are comfortably as quick point-to-point, that the drivetrain is a generation behind the direct competition and that whilst a Ferrari 599 takes its engine from an Enzo the DBS gets its 6.0-litre V12 from a couple of Ford Mondeos. And they'll be right on all counts. But they'll also be wrong, because they'll be thinking with only one frontal lobe, and it's on the left. Aston has a fine grasp of fitness for purpose and well understand that in this rarefied niche it's not what you do but how that's important. ⋮

This car is a stupendous drive and blindingly quick, and if, having driven it, you still feel compelled to go faster on a public road, then it's probably nothing to do with the DBS at all. It may well be a personal issue. Something to do with breast feeding, perhaps, or possibly your relationship with your father.

And the DB5? Well, to drive it's what golfers refer to as a 'son in law' – alright, but not quite what I was hoping for. Some careful upgrades can work wonders on the dynamics, taking them from dangerous to only slightly scary, but the joy of it is that you have a riot while going rather slowly. Recently I've been commuting in it and found it surprisingly good. The sense of occasion you can probably guess,

but the comfortable ride and torquey straight six might surprise you. The real genius of the thing, though, is how it makes you feel. In other cars my commute is a wild-eyed and wired death-battle with cyclists and the eight number 52 buses that move like a North Atlantic convoy down Kensington High Street at 8.30. But in the DB5 I do things like stop in Hyde Park for a coffee (I love this dirty town), look up at the sky and, on one occasion, wave a cyclist in front of me. And all to the evocative soundtrack of a cultured, period straight-six.

The DBS makes a damn fine noise too, mind, apart from at start up, where a compulsory and violent throttle blip makes it sound like Darth Vader being taken by surprise in the prison shower.

It also looks exactly as an updated DB5 should. No Mustang-style retro pastiche here; Aston quite understands both what a classic model like the DB4/5 was all about *and* how to re-interpret it for this millennium. The only possible slip is the glamorous, but over-designed interior. Astons are traditionally restrained inside, but the DBS dash has gone a bit Bang & Olufsen. Instead of a key we get an Emotion Control Unit – well exactly – which, because there's nothing wrong with a key, is patently a cure for no known disease. It also weighs a lot more than a key. It weighs more than a padlock actually, which makes you wonder why they're using super light and very expensive carbon fibre everywhere else. It's the little details.

'This car is a stupendous drive and blindingly quick, and if, having driven it, you still feel compelled to go faster on a public road, it's nothing to do with the DBS'

While the DB5 gearshift is topped by an elegant and compact bakelite ball, the DBS' gear knob looks like a beautifully burnished aluminium rendering of Bigfoot's dick.

My only other reservation with the DBS was a subtle question of identity. Astons are classic, front-engined 2+2 Grand Tourers that do what they say on the tin. Start adding carbon fibre, taking out rear seats to lose weight and talking about lap times, and you risk corrupting the Secret Recipe. There is, apparently, a long racetrack in Germany, which I've never driven on, called the Nobürgersring where people called Manfred drive very quickly, and about 50 people die every year. I really don't care at all how quickly a DBS laps it and I wish Aston

didn't either, but I'm beginning to suspect it does. As one example, Aston Martins have, since the dawn of time, had rear seats – because they are GTs, not sports cars – but the DBS has had them removed to, apparently, save weight. Now I've no idea how much two cushions weigh – probably less than one Emotional Control Unit, come to think of it – but the fact that losing them produces a .217 second reduction in the car's lap time is greatly less important to me than the fact that it's now illegal to take my children anywhere in it. It also, at a stroke, has everyone comparing the DBS with 599s and GT2s, where it is simply out of its depth, instead of the 612s and Continental Speeds that are really the natural competition.

But, hey, don't listen to me. I'm being picky. I loved the thing, and so will you, and the simple fact is that for £160,000 there is no more charismatic or desirable bit of automotive sculpture out there. Would I change my DB5 for it? Of course I wouldn't – like Daniel Craig in *Casino Royale*, you really need both. But, different as they are, they share Aston's greatest weapon. The curse of modern life is that nagging sense we all get of always going somewhere, but never quite arriving. And Aston Martin's secret is that they make you feel like you've arrived.

So there it is. The first published article on Aston Martin for 40 years not to mention the word Bond. Aaagh! Fell at the last. ∎

This is hardcore

The last Focus RS was a disappointment. Not this one. **Jeremy Clarkson** straps himself into Ford's 300bhp monster and goes in search of his inner hooligan

Photography by Joe Windsor-Williams

I'M RELIABLY INFORMED, BY MY 14-YEAR-old daughter, that there are two types of people in the world – Chavs and Sloanes. And there are no prizes for guessing which type will be most interested in the new Focus RS – a car that comes in a choice of three colours: DFS blue, Stiletto white and Bacardi Breezer green.

On the very day production of this new car started in Germany, I took it for a spin up here in the Cotswolds and, frankly, I couldn't find one house outside which it might look even vaguely appropriate. If it were a garden ornament, and it sort of is when it's parked outside your house, then it would be a stone lion and, as a result, I feel fairly sure that if you were to apply the *Top Gear* cool test – would Kristin Scott Thomas like it? – the answer would be: "No thanks. I'll go on the bus."

So let's ignore the Sloanes, shall we, and start off by saying, "Chavs. This one's for you."

I'm the man for the job, because I'm a sucker for flared wheel arches. I've often said that in the same way a man can never be too rich, his wheel arches can never be too flared. And the RS, to accommodate its wider track, has some whoppers.

There's another reason I'm a man for the job, though. I love fast Fords. My first love was a GT40, my first car was a Cortina 1600E and back in the Nineties, I ran two Escort Cosworths. And I've always loved RSes too.

From the X pack Capris through the Escort 1600i to the 150mph Sierras.

That's why I was so quick off the mark with the new car. I wanted to see what it was like. And when it arrived at my house, the aural promise of greatness was unmistakable. Its big exhausts, through which the Palestinians of Gaza could smuggle the entire contents of a zoo, make the sort of rumble that rattle even the most beautifully finished sash windows. I honestly thought as it reversed into my yard that my wife was out there in her Aston. It's low loud. Bass loud. Dog-frighteningly loud.

And then came the crushing disappointment. Despite the enormity of Ford's global operation, they had fitted the steering wheel on the wrong side of the car. The man who had brought it tried to argue that in other parts of the world people drive on the wrong side of the road, but obviously he was covering up for some other bloke's massive cock-up. Wrong side of the road? Whatever next?

Assuming that they get this fixed before the car goes on a sale, and I'm assured they will, the interior is much as you'd expect. Extra dials (which you can't read), a satnav with a woman who cannot be silenced unless you are Steve Jobs, and excellent bucket seats. If you have a tweed jacket in your wardrobe, you will hate it in there. If you do not, you will find it great. ∴

The new-gen RS – at last a car worth the moniker

The new Focus RS is the king of grip and poise

Focus RS now has a 'revo knuckle' Ask James May

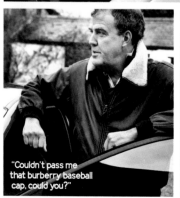

"Couldn't pass me that burberry baseball cap, could you?"

'The engine is epic. Yes, it is essentially the blown 2.5-litre Volvo five-pot from the ST, but with a new, dog-baiting exhaust'

But what about on the road?

The last Focus RS was a huge disappointment. It looked good – better than this one, in fact – but to tame the engine's not particularly stratospheric power, it had been fitted with a front differential of such monumental hopelessness, it probably thought it was a biscuit. You got a ton of torque steer when you set off, then the steering system would jam and then you'd hit a tree, fly through the windscreen and be killed. Technically, engineers called the system 'shit'.

I was hoping, as the new RS produces 300bhp, it would have four-wheel drive. But no. That would have been too expensive to engineer, so they've stuck with a diff. I'm told it's all new, and softer in its responses. In other words, it's designed for people who like to drive on roads and not be killed.

Does it work? Well, because it has a revo knuckle – and if you know what this is, you are James May – the driveshafts always stay level with something or other. This means you can blast one wheel through a puddle and not have the steering wheel wrenched from your hand. It also means the car doesn't follow the camber of the road with anything like the hopelessness of the previous RS.

I have to say that even when the weather is awful, the grip and the poise are excellent. Better than excellent. I can't imagine that even an Evo X is going to pull away. I know for a fact that on a damp road, it would leave my CLK Black for dead. It's that good, and not once did I encounter any of the dreaded tread shuffle that seems to plague the testers on other magazines.

But there's no getting away from the fact that the torque steer is still there. I suppose it's a consequence of putting 300 horses through a system that also has to deal with the steering. It's physics. Get used to it. It's worth it.

The engine is epic. Yes, it is essentially the same blown 2.5-litre Volvo five-pot from the ST, but it has new pistons, a new blower, a new intercooler, a new inlet manifold and that new, dog-baiting

exhaust system. Of course, there's some lag, but from less than 3,000rpm you can feel the shove, you can feel the urgency, you can feel the 324lb ft of torque. And unlike most turbo engines, which run out of puff when you get near the red line, this one keeps right on singing. Well, shouting.

Ford says the ST is like a dolphin, and the RS is like a shark. I'd like to laugh at them for this, but they're right. It's a good analogy.

Except the RS is nowhere near as hard as you might imagine. Of course it's firm, but it's not "Oh Christ. My Teeth!" firm. It's more sort of reassuring.

So let's talk money. The Focus RS costs £24,995, and at that sort of price, this sort of speed and this sort of engineering is unheard of. Especially as it comes with seating for five, a big boot, fold-down rear seats and lots of buttons.

As a result, I wouldn't hesitate for a moment. I'd have a slower but more discreet Golf GTI. But that's because I've moved on. My house is yellow, and my wellies are French. But if you haven't moved on. If your hat is still on back to front. If you still think the Boss is God and your collar's still blue, then trust me: life has never been better. The RS glory days, after a momentary blip, are back.

Are you Stig enough?

We've always thought someone would build a hatch hot enough to fry a supercar. Is the new RS - in Tom Ford's hands - that car? And what happens if the supercar is driven by The Stig?

'Move out of the way, could you Stigster? I'd like to overtake'

'Get three per cent cheeky with the throttle in the GT, and you'll suddenly be aware that you're at the mercy of the car's momentum'

FOR EVERYONE WHO'S BEEN GUILTY of a bit of furtive lechery over the gory details of the new Focus RS, the good news is that you can now pop your head out of the closet, reach for the turbocharged top-shelf pornucopia and revel in a bit of completely unequivocal Fast Ford barminess. The new RS isn't just good, it's *berserk*.

Good. That's that out of the way. Best to deal with the headlines, because so far there's been a fair bit of down-mouthed speculation about the drivetrain. Three-hundred bee-haitch-pee in a front-wheel drive? *Really*? Yes, really. And the new 'Quaife Automatic Torque-Biasing Limited-Slip Differential' or 'QATBLSD' for, um... short, is better than most four-wheel-drive systems. Not all, but most. This front-driver, for example, is more natural and keen in its responses than any Haldex-shod Golf or 4x4 Subaru. Big talk then, but how do we prove it?

A demonstration feels necessary. So hello Stig, and hello Stig-spec white Ford GT, and hello too to the colonic loops of bumpy tarmac above Monaco in the South of France. Me versus It, and It has more power, more skill and less imagination than Me. You might think that I've set myself up for a fall. Nope – that much becomes obvious as soon as I press myself into the RS's hip-huggy Recaros, disengage the traction and give it death in the first three gears after having a peculiar 'go big, or go home' moment. And the immediate verdict is: HolyCrappingHell.

This new Ford Focus RS – with 300bhp and a sophisticated limited-slip diff – is faster than a 500bhp Ford GT on a twisty back road, by some margin. Even though the GT is much heavier than the Focus at 1800-odd kg, we didn't expect the RS to mount such a comprehensive

annihilation of the supercar's point-to-point ability. Cor, and, indeed, blimey.

OK, so I didn't beat the Stig up the mountain – I would dearly love to tell you otherwise and wipe the uncaring smugness off the damn thing's inexpressive helmet – but I would have done if I was, by some quirk of twisted space/time, driving both cars at the same time. And if the route had contained absolutely no straights, because the straights were where the GT pulled out the supercharged V8 joker and did the Millennium Falcon bit. BUT, the big news was that I was closer than anyone, including myself, imagined. So much so that even The Stig itself had the good grace to stare in my direction with what I'm going to assume is bemused surprise when we arrived at the top within a second or so of each other. At least, that's what I'm assuming, given that he apparently still has no idea that I even exist, or why I was there.

So the question is why? First up, the benefits of a familiar backdrop are obvious. Despite the fact that the RS feels like a nicely special thing (wingy seats, bonus boost and oil temp dials, RS-ified wheel, wide stance), it is still, after all that, *just a Focus*. Which means that you can jump straight in and know where the indicators are, how to fill it up with petrol and that you'll be able to tool it around an underground car park without scratching the alloys. That means that even when you open it up and start to discover what kinds of magic have been wrought on the 2.5-litre five-

cylinder turbo engine and FWD transmission, you are still discovering speed from a position of relative relaxation.

The GT never allows you quite the same level of nonchalance. You can't really see out of it, and it feels lorry wide. The supercharger belt is spinning just over your right shoulder, about six inches from your ear, and everything feels unfamiliar. Part of the glory of such a special car certainly, but not a situation in which you can second-guess stuff too easily. The dynamics similarly take much longer to assimilate with the GT; take just one corner that little bit too hard, get that three per cent cheeky with the throttle and you'll suddenly be very aware that you're at the mercy of both the GT's momentum and mid-engineedness. That's not to say that it isn't utterly thrilling to blather along in a GT, but it doesn't flatter to deceive; there is No Traction Control other than your right foot – get it wrong and you'll be going home in a bag. It takes concentration to drive quickly and stepping over the mark will evaporate confidence – the bald truth is that a twitch in a Ford GT means more to your ego, and therefore your confidence, than a twitch in a Ford RS.

The RS allows you to steal precious distance back from the driver of the GT, almost directly out from under his delightfully wide rear bumper, mainly because it rides with supernatural aplomb over properly horrible bumps. Yes, it is a very firm car – but it doesn't crash. Yes, there is an element ⸬

'The RS just loves, *loves* to be thrashed. It revels in being hammered, thrills to the redline and bangs through the gears'

of roll when you turn in from the fantastic – if slightly light – steering, but that initial softness gives the damping – and you – time to settle. It feels like a properly sorted fast road car, rather than a granite-sprung racetrack refugee – which never works in real-world driving. You also need that moment of transition, because from there on in it's pure, hectic, joyous abuse.

The RS just loves, *loves* to be thrashed. It revels in being hammered, thrills to the redline and whooshes, sneezes and bangs down through the gears, sounding like four-fifths of a WRC car. The gearbox isn't its best feature, feeling a little loose at times, and the brake pedal could do with being slightly firmer. But every time you think you can't go any faster, it will surprise you. Slam on the brakes way too late, turn-in way too hard, wallop in the power way too early, and the RS just drills into the corner like it's caught a rut bound for the apex. It goes so hard that if you're on a twisty road it can get faintly concussive.

The smackdown is that it all feels so cohesive, so together, so *easy*. Every time you come to a corner you can eke out several feet more of braking distance simply by knowing that should you turn in and there's something coming the other way you only take up one half of the road; the GT's physical dimensions mean that you occupy about a third too much width to be genuinely comfortable. And the continuing thievery is entertaining – every corner becomes a little nip at the theory that you need to have a thick wallet to go indecently quickly.

It's also a revelation that deploying the 300bhp in the Focus is child's play. You can feed in the power without (thank God) the irritating torque-steer of the old car. The torque will still disrupt the wheel – especially on a full-throttle upchange – but where the old RS would actually change direction with its hard-core diff and therefore require an irritating correction, the new improved RS tugs rather than yanks. You can trim the line with the throttle without any nervous wiggles or snappy reactions. The steering also has feeling, despite the honking great mass of complicated stuff positioned between you and the tyres. You can be more brutal with this car than with anything else I have driven in the past couple of years... and still fire out of a corner the right way round and smiling.

Here's another truth: You have to be a damn sight richer than me to not care that you're driving a big, expensive supercar. The Stig quite blatantly couldn't care less (if indeed he has the capacity to care at all), but for the rest of us there's an element of nervousness, no matter how experienced you are with cars with high net-worth and high horsepower figures. With a £25k Focus, you can push the expensive shininess to the back of your mind more easily, which allows you to just get on and enjoy driving it. The same theory applies to all hot hatches – part of their speed is based on their inability to be intimidating in the same way as a £100k-odd behemoth with a 5.0-litre supercharged V8 that's bellowing a thick, angry aria just behind your ears.

It doesn't matter that the GT has several hundred horsepower more than the RS, it doesn't matter that it can pull more lateral G, or that it is by some margin a more focussed fast car, it's just that in the RS you can deploy 85 per cent of the available ability in every situation. The GT just can't. On any kind of straight, the GT just murders the RS no matter how useless the driver – but it's when you start to pinch back effortless seconds on the bendy bits that the RS starts to make rich owners of supposedly superior cars (at least in terms of RRP) sweat quite badly and have militant thoughts about their latest supercar acquisition.

There is nothing worse than being in a car you know to be several times faster than the one following you, and not being able to lose it. The reason being that, when you tot up all the available information, the driver in the other car is just plain old *Better. Than. You.* This is quite obviously not the case when you try to follow The Stig, whose car control is quite frankly extraordinary no matter what car you point him at, but he should have *murdered* me – and keeping him in sight felt like a massive victory, both for me and the Focus.

So what have we learned? The new Focus RS is a deeply joyous thing. It rewards hard driving with the lairy brilliance that an RS Ford should be all about. But, better than that, it gives up that brilliance early, suffuses the driver with an enormous amount of confidence. And confidence brings speed. The biggest compliment I can give it? It can put an average driver in sight of The Stig in a supercar on a twisty road. Which, let's face it, is as near as you're ever likely to get.

SPEED OF LIGHT

The Caterham R500 will reel in that light at the end of the tunnel in a blur of insane acceleration. Tom Ford prepares to get seriously warped

Photography by James Lipman

'When it spits a foot of blue-tinged orange flame from the exhaust on the overrun - as it will if you're trying even half-hard - you'll be convinced this is a bad motherfunker'

Good design, simply executed - the R500 has 'cool' by the shedload

Seat padding is provided by your own plump rump. Chips it is, then

Seeing as we tested out R500 No 001, surely we should try the rest as well?

BLOOD RUSH. MY HANDS are shaking, my eyes are streaming, my heart is trying to smash its way into my throat. I can hear someone muttering swearwords in my helmet, and it takes a couple of seconds to realise that the mutterer is me. The first time you give Caterham's new R500 Superlight full throttle on a public road, you *will* emerge in a state of shock.

It's obvious that the R500 has stimulated my fight-or-flight, something instinctive from the murky depths of survival-based genetic make-up. Thing is, I'm definitely feeling like prey at the moment, like an exposed meerkat on an open plain near a tree full of starving eagles, and it's not just because this car feels like it wants to tear my head clean off. We're taking pictures of this newest, barest-specification Caterham in London tunnels and backstreets that I wouldn't be comfortable walking down in the blazing day... and it's currently three o'clock in the morning. The crackheads are circling. It's dark and a little bit slippery and nocturnal and weird – it's all getting a little bit medieval. Probably not the best place to try the Caterham's new launch control system.

Ah, sod it.

After a couple of abortive attempts at a fast start and several *very* successful full-bore trials (sorry, Officer), it becomes clear very quickly that there is little on this planet that is capable of providing the unadulterated visceral thrill of a fast Caterham, and if you're going to do it, you might as well go big, or go home. The new R500 weighs just 506kg, has 263bhp from its Ford Duratec 2.0-litre four-pot, and can hit 60mph in 2.88 seconds. Ever wanted to know what 520bhp/tonne feels like when the exhaust is a foot from your right ear and your bottom is plugged into a carbon-fibre bathtub? Well, it's like someone is trying to ream out your skull with the Devil's own hammer drill, that's what it's like.

When it spits a foot of blue-tinged orange flame from the exhaust on the overrun – as it surely will if you're trying even half-hard – you'll be utterly convinced that this is one bad motherfunker. Flames, I decide in one particular tunnel in south London, rule. Thing is, there's not much time to assess exactly why this car is so thrilling, because it's basically one long, drawn-out heart attack on wheels. First and second gears are literally a blur. The acceleration and vibration is so violent that your eyeballs can't compensate. All you do is hold on, and keep one jittery orb pointed in

the direction of the change-up lights mounted just south of the right-hand aero screen.

When you see the final flash of red, lift, pull firmly back on the gearstick and repeat. You can full-throttle upchange with no clutch, but the car seems to unsettle slightly on a cambered UK country road, so a slight lift allows a smoother transition. The gearbox is so connected, so very *now*, that it feels like you're reaching into the gearbox casing and slapping the gears into place with armoured fingers. Like someone slamming a heavy metal door right next to your left thigh.

The physicality of it leaves your fleshy body with no place to hide – there is no seat padding, the Kevlar buckets are approximately 1/8th of an inch thick and weigh less than my last large dinner. Your bottom-fat is the only cushion, hence the insistent vibration, and the rear axle sits around six inches from your backside. You spend the first 20 miles convinced you are about to stick the car into/under/onto the nearest violently debilitating object, until you realise that the squirming and bumping is actually what any car feels like when the sensation isn't filtered through numbing suspension. The difference in feel from this Caterham to something like a Ferrari F430 is the difference between placing your hand on the road and licking it.

Tunnel vision – in some cases, this is actually a good thing, eh, Tom?

The gearbox is an optional sequential six-speed, and utterly in keeping with the violent attitude of the car, although it adds 10kg over the standard manual. You pull back to change up, stab forwards to change down. Reverse and neutral require a pull of the gearstick collar or a push forwards. All very simple, and after a mile or so, you can't imagine why anyone would actually want to have any other gearbox in a fast car. Gears engage with a thump and a clack – the same sound you hear when a big-power superbike engages first at the traffic lights – and after that, you have armed the warhead, and you'd better be ready.

Even though the engine itself is a relatively normal Ford Duratec 2.0-litre, it comes equipped with roller-barrel throttle bodies and is tuned to insanity by Caterham Powertrain (CPT). The maximum power hit of 263bhp arrives at a lofty 8,500rpm, with a low-sounding max torque of 171lb ft coming in at 7,200rpm, when most engines are begging for another gear. The torque figure sounds skinny, but when you remember just how light this car is, it makes precisely naff-all difference to the amount of speed you can unleash with a mere twitch of your right foot.

That gastric-band diet is the thing that allows the R500 to devour the horizon-line. There's a carbon dash, carbon nose-cone and carbon rear and front cycle wings. Caterham has mined several kilos from the R400's featherweight chassis and even the airbox is pure carbon. The ally bonnet is so light you can comfortably pick it up with one finger, and the wheels are tiny 13-inch lightweights, shod with Avon CR500 tyres that can generate enormous grip when hot. I'm not sure that an R500 would be all that much fun in the rain, though – you'd get very wet, and then, if you decided to run out of talent, you'd get very hospitalised.

The suspension is similarly pinpoint and uncompromising. Optional Eibach adjustable springs and dampers, which come straight from the Caterham C400 race series, are at work here. The Avons take a while to get up to temperature, and it takes a little time to get used to the way the car changes direction – basically you have to stop overreacting to the sensations mainlined into you from the chassis and suspension. Put simply, the point at which the R500 is just informing you of what's going on with the back axle and the amount of grip available, is the point at which most fast cars are actually mid-slide and about to crash. Basically, you have to recalibrate your style quickly for the R500, or you spend your time over-driving.

The bizarre thing about the new version of the R500 is that, despite all the hardcore sensation, it's actually very easy to drive. Hard, ultra-connected, low and exposed, but actually pretty easy to trawl about in. The gearbox clacks into gear, and there's a fluffiness to the initial low-rpm response as the induction gets going, but once you're clear of the first 3,000rpm, the engine pulls like you've just been hit up the backside by an artic doing 60mph.

Of course, it's not perfect. The brakes take some getting used to – especially thanks to the tiny pedal box and pedals that all but sit atop one another – so if you go hard you'll be locking up into tighter corners until you get used to squeezing the brakes rather than standing on them. Also, running the

car into town after a cross-country run, it got to the fourth set of traffic lights before flashing up a 'high temperature' warning. A couple of miles later, and I was forced to pull over and cool it down. Considering it was 2am, the clubs were kicking out and the world was full of drunk people trying to hitch a lift, that wasn't exactly convenient. You might think I'm being unfair, but the very fact that the car is so well engineered that it can drive around town so easily means that it feels like a bit of let-down that it can't just keep itself cool. You really could drive this car to the racetrack, beat everything and drive home – if you fit a bigger fan.

This sort of speed and experience also doesn't come cheap. The basic R500 costs £36,995. If you want one like that in the pictures on these pages you need to add the sequential gearbox (£2,950), launch control (£350), suspension pack (£1,250) and the carbon induction kit (£450). That tots up to a not-inconsequential £41,995. Gulp. But for that you get a driving experience unlike any other currently available, no matter the cost. I'm not a big track-driving fan, but realistically that's the only place you'll really be able to see just how brutal and sticky the new R500 really is. On the road, it is merely devastating. But at this point in time, there is no other car like it on the planet. I love it more than is legal, even in the Netherlands.

Here is the wind diffuser. It's not very big. You will need a helmet

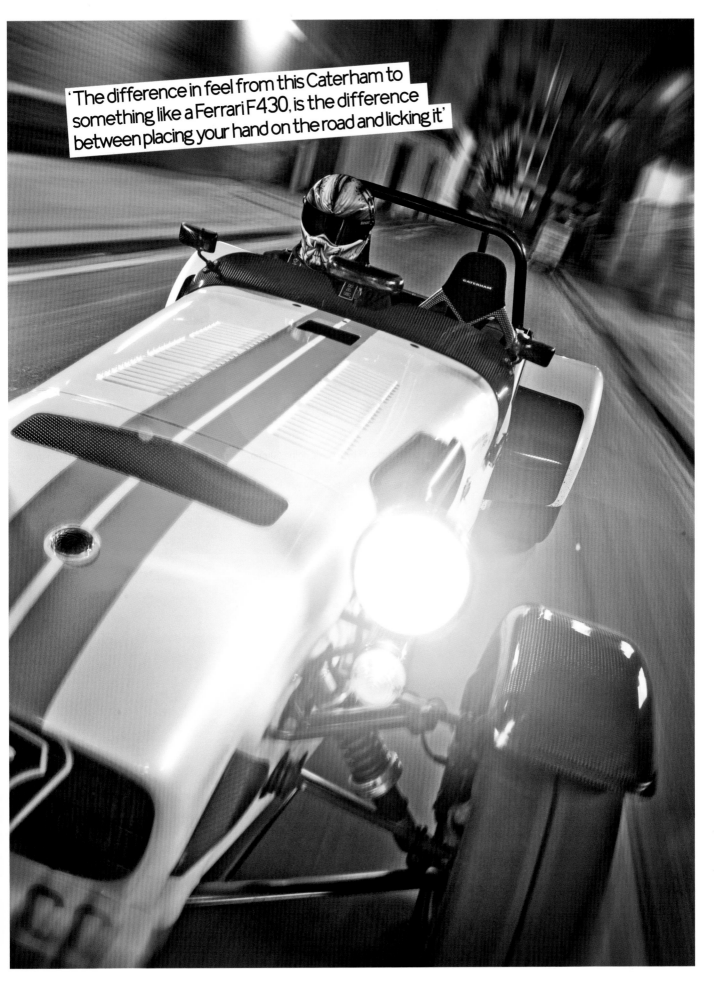

'The difference in feel from this Caterham to something like a Ferrari F430, is the difference between placing your hand on the road and licking it'

England's Dreaming

More than just a sports car company, Morgan stands for
all that's best about Britain and our Hamster should know

WORDS: **RICHARD HAMMOND**   PHOTOGRAPHY: **JUSTIN LEIGHTON**

ON THE FACE OF IT, THERE WAS NOTHING remarkable going on: the owner of a manufacturing business was showing me around his factory with evident satisfaction while talking about plans and technological developments to take the company into the future. Nothing remarkable except that the factory makes cars, the company has been in business for a hundred years and the man showing me round has the same name as the cars themselves: Morgan. And so Charles, son of Peter Morgan, grandson of company founder HFS Morgan, led me around his crazy collection of sheds, purpose-built complexes and cricket pavilions at the Morgan factory, talking passionately about superformed aluminium body panels, bonded aluminium chassis, hand-formed ash frames, wood-jointing and hydrogen fuel cells. He showed me how he is expanding the site, and setting up a museum and showroom adjacent to the factory ready to welcome the swarms of people visiting from all over the world in Morgan's centenary year.

I had visited the factory to drop off my Aeromax for its 1,000-mile shakedown. Those first thousand miles had passed in a thunderous, heart-pounding storm of V8 noise and hard-edged performance. The rose-jointed suspension makes for precision and predictability on the road, the lightweight, rigid structure and 325bhp V8 make for speed and power to push that handling right to the edge. But this isn't some old-school, hairy-chested bit of macho mechanical nonsense here. The Aeromax, along with the Aero 8 Roadster, is every bit the modern car. The aircon, electric windows, satnav, subwoofers and central locking are all incorporated seamlessly into the handmade leather interior – as seamlessly as the bonded aluminium chassis works with the hand-made ash frame to blend the best of old and new and create a time-warping mix of styles, ingredients and techniques. It might look like an escapee from a retro-futuristic movie, but it's very much a modern, usable car. And that shape, that long, low, mean and beautiful shape; we are unused these days to objects ⁘

imbued with such an overt sense of drama and the theatrical – things designed to look sumptuous and exciting, but to do so with an awareness of their own ridiculousness, their unnecessary-ness. The big Morgan is wild, beautiful and crazy but, perhaps above all else, has a sense of humour about itself. And that's the key to it, to how it differs from the typical modern, self-conscious, knowing supercar. There is no tedious, pub-bore obsession with theoretical numbers and track times here; it is happy to be a bit of a cartoon of itself. And as a result, blasting around in it has been an absolutely unique and wonderful hoot.

Yes, there have been a few niggles along the way. The radio aerial doesn't really work, because Charles refuses to let them drill holes in that gorgeous body to mount one, so the guys are investigating other options. And one of the beetle-wing windows at the back refused to rest in the open position properly, thanks to a faulty, but now replaced, hydraulic support. But, overall, I had spent a fabulous fortnight getting to know the big 'Max and was happy to swing back into the factory with it wearing the mud and grime of a busy, happy, hard-charging time along its svelte flanks.

Charles Morgan met me and the filthy Aeromax at the gate, and immediately we set off on one of his impromptu factory tours. We watched the guys building traditional Roadsters, fitting engines into steel chassis and working in the woodshop putting together the wooden frames onto which the aluminium body panels are fitted in the same way that the original coach-builders made horse-drawn carriages three centuries ago. My grandfather worked as a coach-builder at Mulliners, and I inherited from him, if not any discernible talent on a practical level, an appreciation at least of the skills, time and creativity that go into the process of making cars this way. Stepping into the woodshop, seeing the racks of traditional woodworking tools and smelling the resinous air, you could easily imagine you'd wandered into a furniture factory by accident.

A quick trip to the next shed down the row is enough to banish such thoughts. Because here, as Charles explains to me for the thousandth time, is where they build the Aero 8 Roadster and its rarer

sibling, the Aeromax. And here is where the last of the myths concerning Morgans really can be put to bed. Because no, they do not have, and never have had, a wooden chassis. The traditional Roadsters are built on a steel chassis onto which an ash frame is fitted. The aluminium body panels are then fitted on to the ash frame and that, in short, is coach-building. So, no wooden chassis. In fact, the Aeromax and Roadster are based on a bonded aluminium chassis, much like a Jaguar XK or a Lotus Elise. Except Morgan adopted the technique years before Jaguar, Aston Martin and Ferrari followed suit. Some body panels are made using a technique adopted from manufacturers of aircraft jet engines, in which the aluminium is superheated until almost molten before being moulded into shape. It's called 'superforming', and it allows for consistency and accuracy beyond any other system. And it's something Morgan adopted long before Bentley and Rolls-Royce did the same.

We survey the Aeromax and Aero8 chassis under construction. One or two are being fitted with body panels finished in some pretty distinctive colours. It's best not to ask in such a place, these cars are often bought by those who might choose to express their individuality through the medium of their car's colour. Charles is distracted suddenly by the sight of the rear panel going on to another Aeromax. He wonders aloud at the complexity of the shape of this one panel and how it would be ⸭

Rear light (right) is fiendishly expensive to place here

Shiny and clean, this must have been after its shakedown check

'The big Morgan is wild, beautiful and crazy but, perhaps above all else, has a sense of humour about itself. And that is the key to it'

Eating a sausage or three with the gaffer: it could only be Morgan

"Seriously, if you flap these fast enough, you can actually take off"

Add V8 howl and doppler Hammond whoop noise

PETER MORGAN'S OFFICE

These guys have been doing this for 100 years now

Workers watch the trees grow, ready to get going on frames

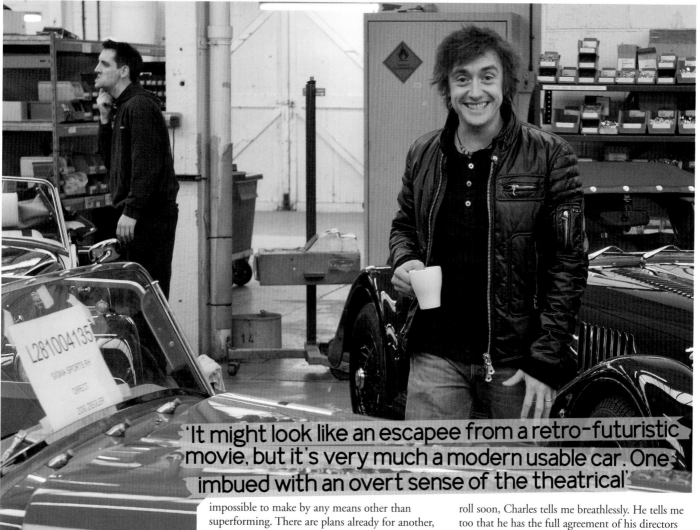

'It might look like an escapee from a retro-futuristic movie, but it's very much a modern usable car. One imbued with an overt sense of the theatrical'

impossible to make by any means other than superforming. There are plans already for another, high-end, limited-edition Morgan, and Charles will unveil it to the world at the next year's *Glamorouse* at the *Concorso d'Eleganza* Villa D'Este in April. They have given him permission to show a concept car. This, though, he assures me with a grin, will be a real car intended to make it into, albeit limited, production, and it will be built in this very plant.

And then he charges into his favourite subject which, unusually for the boss of a car company right now, is the future. Back over by reception, they have the first Life Car, a hydrogen-fuel-cell-powered car that still uses wood and aluminium allied to the latest materials and technology in construction and propulsion. It's not just a pipe dream, it's real, and will be refined and ready to

roll soon, Charles tells me breathlessly. He tells me too that he has the full agreement of his directors and shareholders that this and other projects like it are carried out with the aim of producing a car not to replace the current Morgan range, but to complement and work with it. Charles makes it quite clear that he still wants to shudder with joy to the bellow of a V8 like the one under the bonnet of my Aeromax.

But it is important to look to the future too. He is working with BMW and other partners on future technologies. Though he's not too keen, he tells me, conspiratorially, behind his hand, on the Stop Start stuff, "'cos it sounds so bloody boring". And I laugh because he is the owner of a 100-year-old sportscar company, and he doesn't want to get too tied up with worrying about things that stop and start in traffic when there are broad, leafy roads out there that need to be charged along to the accompanying bellow of a mighty V8 and the tense shudder of a wood-rimmed steering wheel in your grip as the sun sets over the Malverns.

A man arrives at my shoulder. He is wearing blue overalls and carrying a tray. On it is a plate full of sausages.

"Cooked too many of them. From the canteen. Want one?"

Too right. Charles has one too, and the bloke sets off round the factory floor in search of other takers. Morgan. They were there at the start of motoring history, and they'll be there at the end. Whenever that comes. 🔲

A birds-eye view of the Morgan factory. Colourful

WING COMMANDER ANDY GREEN
BLOODHOUND SSC PILOT

'This is an engineering adventure. We don't know exactly what's going to happen. All sorts of things might occur, but they're unlikely to be catastrophic'

WHEN 763.035MPH JUST ISN'T ENOUGH...

In 1997, Wing Commander Andy Green became the fastest man in the world by driving Thrust SSC at 763.035mph. Twelve years later he's back, this time trying to break the 1,000mph barrier

Insane, or just plain British? Either way, we love it...

Story by Jason Barlow Photography by Lee Brir

BEN EVANS
CFD Engineer
"I did feel a certain amount of pressure"

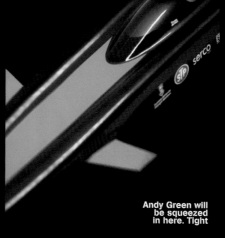

Andy Green will
be squeezed
in here. Tight

DANIEL JUBB
Falcon Project (rocket engines)
"It's somewhere between a racing car and a space rocket"

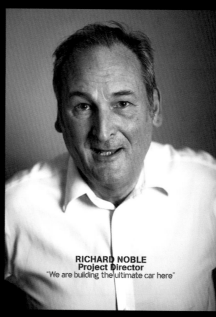

RICHARD NOBLE
Project Director
"We are building the ultimate car here"

JOHN PIPER
Engineering Director
"I don't like the word 'difficult'"

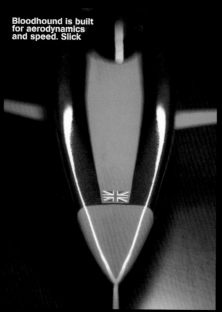

Bloodhound is built
for aerodynamics
and speed. Slick

RON AYERS
Chief Aero Engineer
"A pedantic methodology is the only way"

B

BACK IN 1977, THE STRANGLERS assured us there were 'no more heroes'. Well, they obviously weren't bargaining on Wing Commander Andy Green.

It's impossible to come away from an encounter with the man without being profoundly impressed. Not because he's the current holder of the land speed record – 763.035mph – although that is a deeply impressive achievement. Nor is it because he was an RAF fighter pilot (he's now a 'desk jockey'), although who amongst us hasn't wondered what that must be like as a day job? It's not even because he got a First in mathematics at Oxford University, and therefore must have a brain like a super-computer.

No, it's Andy's ability to process staggering bits of information, then casually fillet them of all the elements that would have 99.9 per cent of humanity running for the hills in abject terror that makes you wonder whether he isn't, in fact, some kind of prototype MoD robo-warrior.

Just as he did in 1997 with the record-beating Thrust SSC, Andy will be driving the new Bloodhound SSC, with the express intention of taking this awesome looking jet engine/rocket-powered hybrid up to and beyond 1,000mph. Yes, 1,000mph. Mach 1.4. On land.

Frankly, strange things are likely to happen at that sort of velocity. The problem is, nobody on the highly qualified Bloodhound team knows exactly what sort of strange we're talking about. This is a journey into the unknown. Andy, meanwhile, is assessing the risk in the way he assesses all risk: with preternatural calmness.

"This is an engineering adventure," he says. "We don't know exactly what's going to happen. All sorts of things might occur, but they're unlikely to be instantaneous or catastrophic. I'm unlikely to enter a wormhole in space and disappear. It's more likely to be, 'hmm, that's a bit odd...'"

A bit odd. He delivers the words with a startling evenness, like he's just ordered a coffee in Starbucks. But then, go online and by the miracle of broadband and youtube you can see for yourself what happens when a jet-powered car veers off-line somewhere between 650mph and 700mph as a trans-sonic shock (ie: when the airflow around the car turns supersonic but only in certain areas) eddies around it, requiring the driver to apply some serious corrective lock. Look at the way Andy's hands work on the wheel, listen to his commentary – done in classic clipped RAF pilot style – and pay attention to his breathing. He sounds about as physically stressed as he would be strolling in a park. It's astounding, mesmerising stuff. That's Andy Green, breaking the sound barrier in a *car*, and he's getting ready to do it all again. Only much faster this time.

Why? Well, the Thrust team – former record-holder and prime motivator Richard Noble, Andy Green, aerodynamicist Ron Ayers and others – were clearly itching for another challenge. The fact that the now sadly departed adventurer Steve Fossett had bought Craig Breedlove's Spirit of America LSR car and was apparently gearing up for an assault on Thrust SSC's record may have motivated them further. But mostly, Bloodhound SSC came into being for one surprising and worrying reason: Britain is running dangerously low on world-class engineers. Over to the boundlessly energetic and enthusiastic Richard Noble.

"Lord Drayson, who buys aircraft carriers and equipment for the Ministry of Defence, told us that he was having terrible problems recruiting engineers for the MoD. Universities may have increased their numbers, but there has been a systemic failure in terms of the numbers of engineers graduating. Previous generations were inspired by great engineering projects like the Spitfire, Vulcan bomber, the Harrier jump-jet, Concorde... Lord Drayson wanted to come up with something that would fire imaginations again, make science, technology, engineering and mathematics exciting.

"We came out of our meeting with him very energised. I was on a high, Andy's eyes were like saucers. This doesn't usually happen after a meeting at the MoD, I can tell you!"

That was back in 2007. Noble, Green and Ayers had been kicking ideas around for at least a year prior to that. Now, with this added educational impetus and some measure of Government support, the team began to get very serious indeed. How best to fire all those hungry minds? One thousand miles per hour sounded like a suitably iconic target, a decent enough step-up from 763mph. Aero genius Ron Ayers reckoned that a pure jet car would probably be all-out at around ∴

'Andy will be driving Bloodhound SSC with the express intention of taking it up to and beyond 1,000mph. Mach 1.4'

800mph, which meant exploring a jet engine *and* rocket propulsion. That's a whole new, spectacular ball game. Was it even feasible? Nobody really knew. Bloodhound SSC would have to remain under wraps until the team's Computational Fluid Dynamics (CFD) experts at Swansea University (see box-out opposite) figured that bit out.

By the summer of 2008, and with the numbers beginning to stack up, it was time to start feeding the other big machine in a project like this: the publicity one. Noble reckoned the budget for the whole operation would be around £10m – excellent value for money, all things considered – and needed to go public to spread the word to the nation's schools, but also to its financial people. In stark contrast to the highly secretive worlds of F1 or the military-industrial complex, Bloodhound SSC was designed to be a collaborative, morale-boosting engineering programme. Everyone would and should benefit. The new information age would spread the word instantly.

On October 23, 2008, Bloodhound SSC was officially a 'go' project. As Lord Drayson commented at the press launch that day, "to achieve the 30 per cent increase in speed [above the current land speed record] will require the largest hybrid rocket motor ever built in this country, major advances in sensor technology to control the car, fresh thinking on fuel efficiency, and a brand new design for the solid wheels generating a radial acceleration of 50,000g." Amongst other challenges...

The car itself is as mind-boggling as you'd expect. It'll be almost 13 metres long, with a minimal cross-section to reduce drag, will weigh around 6.7 tonnes when it's fully fuelled (down to 4.8 tonnes by the end of a run), will feature a fabulously streamlined body made of carbon composite, and is powered by a state-of-the-art jet engine – the EJ200 from the Eurofighter Typhoon – with a hybrid rocket on top of that. Note the future tense: as yet, Bloodhound SSC is little more than a model and some attractive CAD images.

Engineering director John Piper – a man with the Metro 6R4 WRC, Jaguar XJR14 Group C racer, Mondeo BTCC and most recently the JCB DieselMax record-breaker on his CV – is hard at work on the car's configuration.

"We started with three possible layouts," he says, "and we're currently validating the one we've opted to go with. The rules stipulate that the car has four wheels, two of which have to be steered by the driver. The wheels generate two-thirds of the vehicle's drag, and we need to minimise that without compromising on overall stability. Then we develop a shape that can package the components effectively. The jet engine's inlet duct is right in the middle of the car, so that's an issue. As is the weight distribution, and how it alters as the car accelerates to Mach 1.4. As are the wheels, which weigh 140kg each."

As is, well, everything really, which is the whole point. Nobody said it was going to be easy; this is a national engineering adventure, after all. As John Piper wryly points out, "I don't like the word 'difficult'. Engineers like to think that everything can be worked out. We wouldn't dream of releasing Andy on a run if we weren't confident about what was going to happen."

"There are so many variables at work," adds Noble, "that basically you just have to get on with it. We are building the ultimate car here, and every piece of it is being specially designed. As you progress, you have to start shutting the doors on certain things, and you just have to hope that one of the doors you've just shut doesn't have massive ramifications somewhere else."

There are some absolutes, however. With an average of 25,000lb of thrust (roughly, but not exactly, equivalent to 50,000bhp), the sheer power Bloodhound SSC will be able to summon up is one thing, being able to control it quite another. Because the team intend to target 1,000mph in carefully mapped-out increments ("a pedantic methodology is the only way", says Ron Ayers),

moving from 700mph to 800, then 900 and ultimately 1,000mph, the on/off raw power of rocket propulsion simply wouldn't give them enough control. Control is what the EJ200 jet engine supplies, as well as providing sufficient oomph to propel Andy to 300mph, at which point he'll trigger the rocket.

The rocket itself is a hybrid, whose combustion efficiency and relative ease-of-use compared to solid or liquid propellant rockets, makes it more suitable for a land speed record attempt. A brilliant – and extravagantly moustachioed – 24-year-old called Daniel Jubb is the main man here; a keen 'rocketeer' since the age of just five, Daniel left school at 13 to pursue rocket science. He is a magnificent advert for Bloodhound, with an utterly infectious passion for his – admittedly rather complex – chosen field. "We're somewhere between a racing car and a space rocket here. Rockets aren't a totally known quantity, and you're never that far away from a material failure. We'll be working hard to maximise the safety aspect." (That's about all I could really grasp during our 40 minute conversation, to be honest.)

There are bona fide geniuses at work on Bloodhound SSC, yet not only do they need all the help they can get, they're also actively looking for it. Make sure you visit their website (www.bloodhoundssc.com) to find out how you can get involved: *Top Gear* will be following the team's progress closely as they work towards the 1000mph run, most likely at some point in 2011. If you have any interest in engineering, this is for you. If you don't, this is where you get hooked good and proper.

"It's the most exciting thing you can do on God's earth!" says Richard Noble.

'The car is mind-boggling. It'll be almost 13m long, weigh almost 6.7 tonnes and be powered by a jet from a Eurofighter

Mercedes' SLR 722 has a heroic past to live up to. **Paul Horrell** sees how, with some help from McLaren, it's all a little bit of history repeating

>

Mercedes doffs its cap to Sir Stirling Moss with the new SLR 722 Edition, as Paul retraces part of the Mille Miglia route that sealed Moss's status as a hero forever

Photography by Lee Brimble

AT PRECISELY 7.22 ON THE SUNNY MORNING OF May 1, 1955, Stirling Moss screamed away from Brescia in a 3.0-litre, straight-eight Mercedes-Benz 300SLR open sports car. To all intents and purposes it was a Grand Prix machine adapted to have two seats, the passenger being *Motor Sport* journalist Denis Jenkinson. The race was the Mille Miglia, and for every entrant their start time was their race number: hence, 722.

Ten hours, seven minutes and 48 seconds later, they returned. The car was filthy and battered in the bodywork but running like clockwork. The occupants were coated in black brake dust, oil and road grime and caked in the sweat of their labours in that race-car cockpit for the whole of that broiling Italian day.

Between leaving and returning, they had covered 1,000 miles, across the northern plain, down the Adriatic coast to Pescara, over the mountains to Rome, northwards through the hills to Bologna, then back up the straights to Brescia. Oh, sure, the roads were closed for the event, but they were still Fifties' Italian roads, single-carriageway, hardly improved since the war, rough, gravelly and treacherous through the hills. Towns and villages had no bypasses as the route wound around the Piazza Maggiores, the Via Cavours and the Corso Garibaldis, streets lined the whole way with ill-controlled spectators. At potential collision points a few straw bales were placed cursorily about, though whether to protect the drivers or Italy's architectural heritage isn't entirely clear.

Now do the sums. Moss drove those 1,000 miles at an average speed, all stops included, of nearly 98mph. The car was geared for 170mph on the straights, so that's what he did, for miles on end, arrowing along narrow roads with nothing but trees, rocks and buildings at the sides, and if the road

went straight through a village then so did he. At 170mph. And he took pretty well every one of the corners, whether 120mph sweepers, town junctions or tail-out mountain hair-pins (of which there were thousands) somewhere beyond the limit. He made these unimaginable speeds in a car on drum brakes and crossply tyres, innocent of any kind of power assistance, driver aids or safety feature. Seat belts? They preferred to be thrown clear. And sorry to labour this point, but he kept up this heroic pace for 10 solid hours. And he beat the deity of the day, Fangio, in an identical car, into second, *by a clear 30 minutes.*

Was it the greatest single drive in the history of motorsport? You come up with a better one, then, because if you thought Sir Stirling Moss OBE was just the amiable face of those public-information ads on erectile dysfunction, let the Mille Miglia put you straight. And the four straight times he was runner-up in the Formula One World Championship. And the fact that a generation of British policemen, on stopping any male driver for speeding, were contractually obliged to ask, 'And who do you think you are, Stirling Moss?'

But, of course, Moss had a team behind him. He and Jenkinson had recced the route many times, and Jenkinson had graded every bend. Because this was the 1950s, old chap, there were 'saucy ones', 'dodgy ones', and 'very dangerous ones'. He'd marked every hazard, and noted each blind brow with the potential for taking it flat. He'd transcribed this all onto a roll of paper, winding it as the race progressed past the window of a rainproof box, and communicated the knowledge to Moss with a set of 15 well-rehearsed hand signals. This was effectively the first use of pace notes in the sport, and Moss and Jenkinson knew it would be the only way to beat the Italians in their Maseratis and Ferraris with ⋰

Moss on The Mille...

Keeping up with Stirling isn't possible, even in this SLR...

The Mille Miglia was so unlike circuits, Moss says, and not just because you couldn't learn it all. "You couldn't see the apex of any of the corners because of the wall of spectators. You couldn't go for the perfect line. So you went in on oversteer then if it tightened or widened you could adjust your line using power. The 300SLR was a difficult car to drive but the tail did move, it really bit. That was why it was so good."

How did he keep going for 10 hours? "Youth [he was 24], bravado, adrenaline from overtaking all the cars that had left earlier. Jenkinson and I egged each other on. And Fangio gave me a pill... don't know what it was."

So would the new SLR have done the course as quickly? "It jolly well should have. The 300SLR could corner at 0.75g. The new one will do more than 1g. And the brakes are better. But it wouldn't be so exhilarating because the exhilaration of the 300SLR was in exceeding its limits." Fifties' racers actually enjoyed driving.

From Rome to Siena, Moss was pretty well on his 100mph average. I did it at less than 45mph. OK, I had traffic. But there was a glorious 45 miles in the middle where I had a clear run of sweepers and straights and the twisty Raticosa pass. It took 45 minutes at 60mph. Yes, Moss was a hero beyond imagination.

Still, I did it in half an hour at 85mph back to the airport in a Smart ForFour diesel rentacar. That's autostrada for you.

1. Moss and his navigator Jenkinson powering through Italian roads and avoiding spectators

2. Badge matches race number

3. Red rims round dials, original SLR's were blue

4. Spoiler acts as airbrake and flips up under hard braking

5. Only 150 will be made, so look for the special edition tags on the consoles

6. Grille is a blend of old and new

greatest piece of motoring journalism ever.

And the pair had Mercedes-Benz behind them, too, the mightiest, most thorough, most impeccable team in motor racing in that era.

Which is why we're back on the Mille Miglia course five decades later. Mercedes-Benz and McLaren cars are to build 150 of an even faster version of the mighty SLR called 722. Given that they're mining this seam of history, it seemed the least we could do was to photograph it in that context.

But I have questions. Firstly, is the SLR, in many ways one of the more sybaritic of the modern hypercar generation, really a car that deserves to wear those epic and historic numerals? Secondly, given a modern SLR and the same roads, can we gain any kind of inkling of Moss's heroism? The 722 edition being deemed too precious (and low) for this mission, I take instead a 'regular' SLR, if £317,610 and 626bhp can fit anybody's definition of 'regular'. So it comes to pass that two trucks converge across the Alps on a night-time Italian car park. And both of them have SLRs inside.

The 722 edition has been designed to work better at really big track speeds; the aero gives more downforce, and the low-ered, stiffened chassis set-up cuts roll for even more ultimate grip. You can see the wind-tunnel work as a giant, jutting front splitter. The rear spoiler is recalibrated, to poke higher into the airstream when activated into a 'high downforce' position. As with the standard car, it also flips up almost vertically when you brake hard, so the rear tyres can take more of the braking load. The 722's special 19-inch wheels are crammed with an even bigger pair of front discs.

Its 5.5-litre AMG supercharged V8's output is up from 626 horsepower to 650. Small in percentage terms, admittedly, but given the weight has been cut 44kg to 1724kg (still a lot), the 0-62 time has gone down from 3.8 to 3.6 seconds. Top speed is 211mph. This is a shatteringly fast car in every way. The weight cut comes because a few of the remaining non-carbon pieces in the body have been replaced in that material, and the damper bodies, oil tank and wheels are lighter too.

The SLR's structure is almost entirely of carbon fibre yet you don't see much of the material, except for the seat shells and if you poke about under the boot carpet. The dashboard garnish is aluminium and unforgivable plastic fake aluminium. Now the 722 edition gets carbon dash trim and suede for the seat and steering wheel, stitched in red thread. The only functional difference is the addition of a lap-timing computer.

a great disadvantage. I wouldn't fancy the 722's front splitter's chances on some of the rough roads coming up, and I sus-pect the slightly softer suspension of the regular car – hey, it's hardly soggy – will allow the tyres to work better given we're not on a smooth racetrack. Aerodynamics tuned for 200mph aren't vital on single carriageways either. At least not for me. Moss in '55 could doubtless have made good use of them.

Fruitless to do his whole thousand miles today. The northern part through Ferrara and Padua is hopelessly busy, strip development having crept along most of those old high-ways. So it's by turns impossible or colossally irresponsible to try to match Moss's velocities on open roads. The coastal bit from Ravenna is likewise too built-up, and the section from Pescara inland is more empty but so full of blind bends your speed is limited by what might be coming the other way – especially as you've got to stick to one side of the road not use both like Moss could. Ditto for the route's two most famous mountain passes, the Futa and Raticosa between Florence and Bologna. Moss did those 60 miles in 61 minutes; at just 60mph a slow section for him, but to the rest of us that would be speed to the point of delirium.

No, the interesting leg is through Lazio and Umbria. I start on the outskirts of Rome, end at Siena. The route in 1955 was actually simple. There weren't any motorways, so they used the old national network, roads with evocative names rather than numbers. Via Emilia, via Aurelia, via Salaria, via Flaminia. And for me today, all the way on the via Cassia.

To begin with I'm bottled up through interminable suburbs. A healthy jogger could beat our first 20 minutes. The SLR doesn't care much for it either. Never mind the automatic 'box, leather-lined cab, electric seats and steering column, climate and telematics, it still feels like a thinly draped race car. A Bugatti Veyron is better tamed in traffic. So's a 599; the SLR in many ways feels more like a Carrera GT. The McMerc's super-rigid carbon tub creaks and bangs and the electronically controlled carbon brakes have horrible low-speed modulation. They're either on or off, and the pedal has no feel. The steering is heavy and equally dead. The engine rumbles and zizzes a little. The car's width is a problem, though not an insurmountable one because visibility itself is fine.

Oh, but it makes the school kids' day. This one is painted dark grey but any SLR has such immense presence, it's a shaft of light in the dreary traffic. Yet oddly the SLR has slipped ⋗

It's supercar country
in excelsis Yet a bond never
quite develops.
The car
remains strangely unsubtle to me

1. Carbon interior, suede 'wheel and seats give the best in luxury

2. Brembo brakes and even bigger wheels this time round

3. New front splitter increases downforce at high speed

4. SLR: Sportlich, Leicht, Rennsport. Three words with a lot of history

5. Supercharged V8 gives 0-100km/h in 3.6 seconds.

6. Vents and grilles echo Moss' 722 racing car

out of the general petrolhead consciousness since it launched. Doubters say it's just an expensive SL55. But seeing one and being in one gives lie to the notion. Its presence is one thing that's on a wholly different level from the SL. Its performance, its entire feel and animus, is another.

Towards Viterbo I'm beginning to get an idea of how. There are odd gaps in the traffic. The SLR is a sledgehammer of an overtaker. There are just five speeds, but with 575lb ft of torque from 3,250-5,000rpm, you hardly need more. Kick it down or use the responsive little paddles and there are times when the traction control flickers even at 70-plus. And that's even going in a straight line.

The mighty V8 rumbles deep like NASCAR, then when the supercharger kicks in there's an overlaid scream that fair terrifies you the first time. Then wind down the window for an extra twist: hissing pulses of exhaust from the storm drain side-pipes. I keep shifting up at 6,000-odd, forgetting it'll run to seven. You'd need an autobahn or a track to consistently make use of that top-end, never mind the extra ponies of the 722. Then it's a distant dream, as I'm stuck in traffic for an hour.

Just north of Lake Bolsena, I go through a whole little town at 30mph with no one in front of me. Opening up ahead is some of Europe's best driving country. The view is clear, not only of one of the planet's loveliest landscapes but also of the road as it snakes away. The topography is rumpled like an unmade bed, the road often changing direction in all three dimensions at once. The SLR's performance compresses it, turning what look like straights into bends, sharpening each corner and bringing it closer to the last.

And the SLR eats corners. The V8 sits behind the axle line, so it turns instantly like a mid-engined car, though you experience it differently because your vantage point is so far aft. There is never the sensation of running wide at the front; the only commotion is at the battle of the titans down at the rear contact patches; vast traction versus all that torque.

The suspension's long travel is beautifully judged, the hard town ride morphing at speed into something that'll allow the tyres to follow the convolutions of these road surfaces. You feel it as traction and especially under the violence of hard braking, where the stopping is so true you feel calm enough to glance in the mirror and see the air brake pop up.

So on I bound, along ridges, through valleys, between hilltop towns, up and down the zig-zag pass at Radicofani. It's supercar country *in excelsis*. Yet, all the way, a bond never quite develops. The car remains strangely unsubtle to me. I never doubt its limits, nor the ability of its ESP to sort me out if I exceed mine, but I keep looking for, and not finding, the subtleties of a Pagani, or Ferrari 599 – which has similar power and weight and costs little more than half.

The SLR's steering has no feel. None at all. You can go take a 180-degree bend, steadily increasing power until the grip goes, and never does the rim's weight in your hands alter. It gives no clue about the surface beneath, and making a smooth turn-in is a real challenge. The brake pedal stays wooden most of the time too, which makes me think this is a strangely binary car. It's either cornering or not, braking or not. I suspect that's OK for race drivers because they exist beyond the need for those subtleties of feedback. They know what a car is doing, and just need high limits, in which respect the SLR obliges mightily. I need more feel, and maybe the new 722 will provide what I'm looking for.

So, yes, this is indeed a car fit for heroes. Certainly it's worthy to wear the badges 'SLR' and '722'. I guess that makes me the only unworthy one.

No, Mr Bond, I expect you to drive...

It's *Goldfinger* revisited, as *Top Gear*'s own **Paul Horrell** and **Bill Thomas** recreate the book's famous Rolls/Aston car chase with the new Phantom Coupe and DB9

THERE'S A MOMENT IN IAN FLEMING'S *Goldfinger* when the villain departs in that yellow Rolls-Royce Silver Ghost. The car 'sighed away'. The Ghost was knocking on for 40 years old when Fleming was writing, and that was itself a further five decades ago. Yet that description, 'sighed away', is exactly what happens when you touch the throttle on a Phantom Coupe and notice that by imperceptible silent magic you're underway, even though you couldn't identify the moment when the static condition gave way to one of motion. The Phantom Coupé is a properly modern car, but there is a lot about Rolls-Royce that has never changed.

So we decided on a bit of play-acting. In the book, Bond chases Goldfinger to Geneva in an Aston DB3. In the 1964 film, the cars are updated to a Phantom III and a DB5. We've done our own bit of updating by going for the new Royce and a freshly face-lifted DB9. We start at the point where the freight plane landed at Le Touquet airport. Sorry, though, I have no intention of taking Bill to a torture chamber and threatening to slice him in two if he doesn't spill the beans, and, as far as I know, he isn't out to crack open my evil empire. We're just out to enjoy the trip.

Goldfinger's Ghost was huge. He'd told everyone it was heavy because it was armoured, remember, whereas in fact he replaced its aluminium panelwork with white gold to smuggle the stuff out of the country. The Phantom Coupé is also, when you walk up to it, OMG big. High, for a start. Don't be fooled by the word coupe – you're on a level sightline with people driving Range Rovers. And it's 5.6 metres long. When you arrive at an autoroute toll barrier, be careful not to draw quite level with the ticket-dispenser. If you do, the Spirit of Ecstasy, way up ahead, will kiss the barrier.

The design makes more of the size. The smallness of the windows and lights exaggerates the acreage of metal. And what metal: don't you love that brushed-steel bonnet flowing back from the grille.

The vault door swings open on its rear hinges, making entry untroubled. No need to grunt to shut it; just touch a button, and an electric butler draws it closed. Welcome to one of autodom's finest interiors. Even the front seats are like club sofas – none of that go-faster side bracing. Take things steady in this car and you can still get along briskly. The gentle giant of a V12 idles softly enough that you can be fooled into thinking it's off and re-pressing the start button.

What's glorious about this cabin? In no particular order: polished ash-trays that emerge like drums from the doors. Umbrellas concealed in the front wings. Art Deco cinema mood lighting. The fibre-optic starlight headlining (an option, but why ever wouldn't you?). The solid clunk of the light switch. The astonishing stereo sound. The chrome and laquered wood surrounds to the windows where normal cars just leave an exposed rubber seal. The organ-stop vents with electrical shutter servos. The door mirrors, which have a chrome finisher around the glass where any other car just leaves an unfinished edge.

Your eye alights on these details as experience mounts up. There's so much to get to know on this car. And, to be fair, some of it is misery. The satnav, normally hidden away behind a clock panel, is one of the most user-unfriendly of any car on sale, thanks to awful latency and a clunky 1.0 iDrive controller.

But I know the way. I drive more miles in France than England most years, and never did they slip under a car with as little effort on my part as they do now. The Coupé isn't entirely silent at speed; there's a bit of wind noise. It isn't perfectly, perfectly stable on ∵

The Coupés size is hard to grasp: it's bigger than most bridge piers

The Phantom's rear light cluster is roughly the same size as a phone box

OUANES - CUST

'When you walk up to it, the Phantom Coupé is OMG big. High, for a start. Don't be fooled by the word 'coupé' – you're on a level sightline with people in Range Rovers'

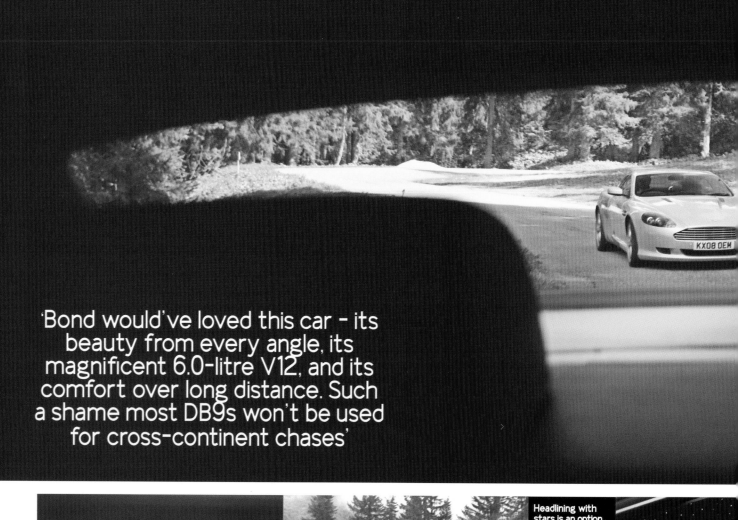

'Bond would've loved this car – its beauty from every angle, its magnificent 6.0-litre V12, and its comfort over long distance. Such a shame most DB9s won't be used for cross-continent chases'

"Ah, Mr Bond. I haven't been expecting you. I've got no booze, nuts, nothing. Sorry"

Headlining with stars is an option. Shooting stars are a further option

the big straights, though it's ruddy good. But there's something about the way it holds itself. There's a near fathomless well of torque (the power-reserve gauge reads 80 per cent remaining untapped at 85-odd mph). The ride, on adaptive air suspension, is always untroubled, even if not meringue-soft. The steering is very low-geared – you take roundabouts and tight corners with huge movements from the shoulders, not wristy little flicks – but every millimetre of rim motion is translated into action, so straight-line running is dead easy. The sheer space around your body encourages deep, relaxed breathing.

More than that, an agreeable feeling of entitlement sweeps over you. Good-natured entitlement, mind, not at all like the arrogance a big, fast SUV tends to engender. So I feel OK about checking into the château at the end of day one. Hey, Goldfinger stayed in nice places *en route*, while Bond hung back at the railway hotel. I get a text from Bill asking how the meal is. 'Beyond five-star,' I truthfully reply. The beep comes back: 'Two-star doesn't begin to describe this shit-hole.'

And it didn't. It was distinctly zero-star. While Paul dined in the château, I was close to the railway station in Reims, tucked away in a grotty little block beyond a dusty park, some way from the town centre. But it mattered not, because a new Aston Martin DB9 was parked in the railway station's long-term car park, strategically placed outside my window. When I

was awakened twice by goods trains in the night, and again by commuter trains and platform announcements in the morning, I pulled back the curtains and admired the silver DB9's sleek shape as it sat there, waiting for another day of Grand Touring.

Bond would have loved this car – its sheer beauty from every angle, its magnificent, high-revving 6.0-litre V12 and its comfort and relative quietness over long distances. Such a shame that most DB9s won't be used for this purpose, chasing across continents at high speed. The car is most comfortable at about 120mph. Where legal...

As I tailed Mr Horrell's Phantom the next day, I had many hours to enjoy the DB9's revised interior. Ergonomically it's a big improvement, but there are still some dreadful niggles that Q would never have let through his net. Sure, Bond would have liked the electric-powered nav screen that emerges from the top of the dash, but he'd have been less pleased to note that it's an old Volvo-based system, at least three years out of date and very clunky. Aston needs to get into bed with a high-end nav outfit. Bond's iPod Touch wouldn't have charged when he plugged it in. That would have pissed him right off too. As would the nav control toggle switch on the dash, which doesn't twist, so you need to find a menu to alter the zoom. At night, he'd have fumbled for a moment for window and mirror switches in the doors that aren't lit, and ⋮

The Aston tries some basic spying by trying to hide behind plant pots

he would have had a quiet chuckle at the 'power, beauty, soul' message that appears on the instrument LED when you push the key fob into the dash. In a Sean Connery drawl: 'Wot ish zish marketing bull-shhhit?' It's an Aston Martin. It doesn't need it.

Still, eliminating those niggles is only a quick squeeze of the throttle pedal away. A mighty V12 bellow, a surge of accelerative force, and chassis, steering and brakes to match. I thought of a passage in the book that made perfect sense as we lanced across N roads near Mâcon...

'In May, with the fruit trees burning white and the soft wide river still big with the winter rains, the valley was green and young and dressed for love.' And it looked even more special through the windows of a DB9...

A Phantom Coupé is shorter by a foot in the wheelbase compared with the saloon. It also has – compared with the Drophead Coupé as well as the saloon – a firmer suspension set-up, slightly reduced steering assistance and an 'S' button that livens the transmission programming usefully. But does all that transform it into a sports car fit for tearing up these hills? Not on your life.

For a start, it's two and a half tonnes. The aluminum space frame is weight-efficient at half a tonne, then there's half a tonne of powertrain and a similar mass of suspension and other mechanicals. That means literally a tonne of luxury. There are vehicles that can corner hard with this sort of height and weight, but they tend to be extreme SUVs with punishing suspensions. Despite its marginally firmed-up chassis, the Phantom Coupé is far from punishing, with the inevitable result that it, well, Rolls: the thing heels into sharp corners like a galleon, and the way you twirl that big wheel is a bit nautical too.

And yet the steering is precise, and it's properly fast: 0–60 is 5.6 seconds, during which that V12 clears its throat and its voice rises slightly. On normal twisting roads, the Coupe makes a decent account of itself.

Monumental R–R Phantom chased by lithe and lovely Aston DB9

'The Phantom Coupé heels into sharp corners like a galleon. And yet the steering is precise, and the car itself is properly fast – 0-60mph in 5.6 seconds'

120 140

100

80

60

40

20

km/h

002974

0

'What's glorious about this cabin? In no particular order: polished ash-trays that emerge like drums from the doors. Art Deco cinema mood lighting. An astonishing stereo'

Wing mirrors on Phantom Coupe are about the size of silver platters

So does a regular Phantom. And here we come to my tiny beef with the Coupé. In pursuit of an unnecessary change in dynamics, something has been lost. The Phantom saloon has the best low-speed ride of any car, and the best supression of high-speed shudders. The Coupé doesn't. So even though overall it still rides mighty well, an element of the unique Rolls-ness has been lost.

But there's no shortage of Aston-ness in the 'new' DB9. It feels solidly made and brutally fast, and its glorious V12 is one of the very greatest powerplants in any car. As I shadowed PH, I wondered whether any car could transport a character like James Bond across a continent with such style, grace and immense pace. The answer is, surely, no. Bond would crave the clear, white-on-black instruments of his old DB3, and some of the interior's classic functionality, but little else. Bond – and Fleming himself – would have loved this car, not least because it is three times more powerful than a DB3. I couldn't wait to jump in the DB9's red seat, set the satnav for 'London' and just drive.

Like a Rolls or an Aston, much about France and Switzerland remains the same all these years on from the 1959 book. The descriptions of the characters of the different towns – Orleans, Maçon, Geneva – ring uncannily true. But, also like the cars, much has changed. There are autoroutes now. When Bond set off to chase Goldfinger, he was on the old high-cambered single-carriageway N1. His car had cross-ply tyres and drum brakes and 'he took no chances'. Yet he covered 43km in 15 minutes. That's a 107mph average. The old Rolls topped out at around 50mph. Back then, because traffic and speed limits weren't the limiting factors, the car you drove made a big difference to your progress.

Today, as long as you can make a steady 90mph, the speed that trips the Gendarmerie's radar on the autoroutes, and you have a decent fuel range, any car will get you from Le Touquet to Geneva in under seven hours. Time doesn't matter any more. The issue is *how* you do the trip.

Because of that, the car still matters. And by the end of it, we adored this Phantom Coupé. Oh, that's not to say we didn't at the start, because this thing certainly makes a mighty first impression. But that impression only deepens when you truly get under its skin.

Expect to see them in the next Hackett brochure

The rest
of the world

Japan and America know how to build fast cars. The muscle car was born in the USA and they still do them better than anyone else: witness the Viper in this section and the Corvette ZR1 in the next, two of the most spectacular and exciting cars on the road.

Japan is synonymous with cutting edge high tech and for car fans that means 'Skyline' – it's called GT-R now but Nissan's new world-beater represents the pure essence of the Japanese supercar.

France, Holland and Sweden make an appearance here too, and if you think their cars lack pace, aggression and ability, think again.

Wanna lift?

Forget all that you think you know. The GT-R hasn't just moved the goalposts, it's obliterated them. **Bill Thomas** is overwhelmed

KAZUTOSHI MIZUNO, NISSAN GT-R CHIEF vehicle engineer, describes his car as a "new kind of supercar, one with no competitors", and I thought of Mizuno-san as I nailed the GT-R's alloy throttle pedal right to the floor in second gear coming onto a quiet section of de-restricted autobahn near Koblenz.

I'd nailed that throttle pedal right to the floor a number of times already on this day – difficult to resist – but somehow the big Nissan seemed to lunge forward with even more intensity than usual. In my imagination, it was sniffing the long, gently-curving, slightly uphill stretch of 'bahn and contemplating the lack of legal restriction on ultimate speed. The only limit would be the power of the car to overcome resistance, and the driver's ability to negotiate traffic. Long may the derestricted autobahn continue: in dry, crisp, sunny conditions, this magnificent car would be safe and composed at any speed.

A bellow from the engine, a rush of revs, a gigantic accelerative force on my neck, second is gone, a flick of the right-hand, leather-trimmed shift paddle, bang, third gear slammed home and the mighty rush intensified still. My god, this car is fast, one of the fastest production cars ever made.

And so's the gearchange. Fast, that is. I could never describe the new GT-R without giving a nod to its incredible transmission right away. Mounted on a transaxle at the rear of the car for better weight balance, it is the technical highlight here. In 'Normal' mode, the shifts from the twin-clutch semi-auto gearbox are rapid, with each pre-selected gear engaging in an instant, but in R mode they're even quicker. We're in R now, and we've hit 100mph in about 10 heartbeats. No official performance figure

exists for that increment, but expect an eight second 0-100mph time. It's fast, alright – 60mph comes up in 3.5 seconds, the standing quarter mile in 11.7 seconds and it goes on to 197mph.

The GT-R's all-new VR38 engine, a 473bhp 3.8-litre V6 with twin IHI turbochargers, makes a fine noise, like a deeper, more muscular 350Z V6 howl overlaid with a harsh, white-noise static blast from the turbos. It is quieter and more gentle in character than the classic RB26 2.6-litre straight-six fitted to Skyline GT-Rs of old, and will probably never be as fondly regarded as a result, but there can be no arguing with its ability to rev, and no criticism of its power delivery. It is entirely linear, with no lag.

Bang into fourth. What a monstrous gear this is, a killing gear if ever there was one. There's no let-up in G pressure forcing my spine rearwards as the tacho needle climbs to the 7,000rpm redline. I have no idea what speed we're doing now, probably upwards of 150mph – I daren't take my eyes off the road.

Bang into fifth. Speed still piling on, the two-lane 'bahn taking on an alarming narrowness which multiplies exponentially for every 10mph you do over 170mph, the barriers closing in, the view beginning to blur to an extent you're not familiar with. A truck flits by on the inside lane, speed difference about 120mph.

Bang into sixth. Getting hairy now. It wasn't until we hit an indicated 190mph that *Top Gear* Creative Director, Charlie Turner, driving the canary yellow Porsche 911 Turbo glued to my tail, flashed his lights impatiently, sick of waiting. Mizuno-san reckons it doesn't exist, but we thought we'd try to find a competitor anyway... ⋮

White lenses in the rear lights just add to the Stig's excitement. Maybe

Switches control (l–r) transmission, suspension and traction control

Steering wheel includes switch for stopwatch. Stig appreciated it

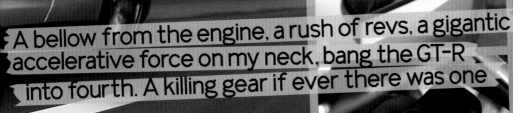
A bellow from the engine, a rush of revs, a gigantic accelerative force on my neck, bang the GT-R into fourth. A killing gear if ever there was one

Seats are superb, include obligatory holes for full race harnesses

You can't change gear with this, just choose which mode you're in

New V6 doesn't have the character of old straight six, but still sensational

It's not space-age design, but it's well made, well finished and functional

The GT-R is all aggression on the outside. To my eye, it is a phenomenal-looking machine, distinct from anything else. Very Japanese and very hard

Dials are classic white on black: LED gives trip info and warnings

The Nissan isn't beautiful and isn't meant to be. Note bonnet Naca ducts

Centre console is a tad plasticky but well laid-out and easy to use

More on the mighty Porsche later. Let's look at the star of the show first, Nissan's new flagship, the brand-halo supercar designed to be sold globally and showcase Nissan's technical skill.

This is not a Skyline, though it's difficult not to call it that. We know the super-quick Nissan in the UK as a Skyline, but in Japan the Skyline is a fairly ordinary four-door saloon with a two-door coupe sister – both are sold as Infiniti G35s in the USA. Nissan has now dropped all links with the Skyline name, because this new GT-R is new from the ground up. Brand new, purpose-built chassis, brand new engine, brand new transmission, brand new body and design. 'Skyline' just isn't good enough.

The GT-R is all aggression on the outside. To my eye, it is a phenomenal-looking machine, distinct from anything else. Very Japanese and very hard. The overall stance is all wide shoulders and slashing arcs, a ground-hugging, flat-sided brute. The aerodynamic performance of the car is astonishing. It has a drag co-efficient to match that of a Prius at 0.27, so the shape is exceptionally slippery. Part of that is down to careful underbody design – a rear diffuser helps generate downforce at speed, too.

Step inside and you're instantly reminded of older Skylines. The design is functional rather than beautiful, quite old-fashioned and not trying too hard, with a large centre console angled toward the driver and a high instrument binnacle across from a large multi-function screen. It all seems superbly well screwed together, as you'd expect of a Nissan, and the quality of the materials is high. It won't win design awards, but I really like the cockpit of this car.

Slot in behind the steering wheel and immediately you feel comfortable and relaxed – this isn't a strange, wide, low supercar, it isn't daunting in that way.

It's much more like a normal saloon in feel. As we'll see, this easy-to-drive nature is a key component of the new GT-R. Keyless entry means you only punch the red metal starter button behind the gear lever to fire up the big V6. With the engine ticking over with a deep burble, you bring the stubby lever back to A-M – it is a normal gate for an auto. Flick it to the right and you have manual, but I want to trundle out of here in automatic first.

The transmission clunks and clacks a bit, but you soon get used to it. Its low-speed manoeuvring isn't on a par with the auto-clutch unit on the F430 Scuderia, being slightly jerky in the uptake, but it's useable. On the move in auto mode, the gearbox is sublime, changing up early in the style of an Audi DSG and using the engine's torque to the full.

We burble out of Nissan's testing facility at the Nürburgring to meet the Porsche, bound for some of the best A-roads in the area, followed by the 'bahn. You will have noticed by now that The Stig appears in these photographs. He materialised from a forest somewhere near Nitz, stood in the middle of the road and held up his hand for us to stop. I then rode shotgun as he thraped the GT-R for 20 minutes, absolutely flat-out, saying nothing. He then stopped and walked into another forest near Fensterseifen.

I have no idea how The Stig got to Germany, but Turner and I brought the Porsche 911 Turbo. Good yardstick, this. As we dispatched the low countries at an easy gait, driving overnight across deserted highways, it seemed inconceivable that Nissan could design anything to get even close to this car.

It is ancient. By 'ancient' I don't mean old-fashioned, other than in its strangely narrow cockpit and upright windscreen – it's ancient in its utter solidity and feeling of being honed for decades. ∴

The GT-R MFD

The Multi Function Display in the new GT-R has 11 separate screens, four of which you set yourself. Within those four, you can choose engine water temp; engine oil temp and pressure; transmission oil temp and pressure; boost; speed; fuel/range; fuel flow; instant consumption; front torque; accelerator, brake and steering inputs; cornering, acceleration and braking G; a G circle, and last but not least, a clock. Enough eh? Phew.

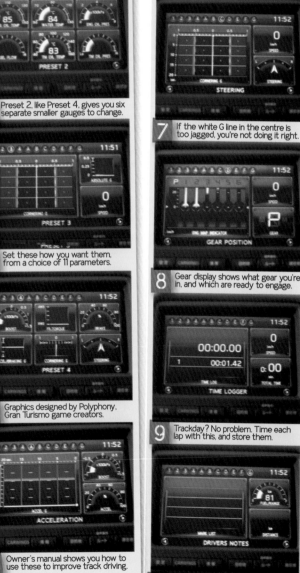

1 Preset 1, like Preset 3, features one large gauge and two to the right.

2 Preset 2, like Preset 4, gives you six separate smaller gauges to change.

3 Set these how you want them, from a choice of 11 parameters.

4 Graphics designed by Polyphony, Gran Turismo game creators.

5 Owner's manual shows you how to use these to improve track driving.

6 A to G are fixed screens. You can't alter the dials on these.

7 If the white G line in the centre is too jagged, you're not doing it right.

8 Gear display shows what gear you're in, and which are ready to engage.

9 Trackday? No problem. Time each lap with this, and store them.

10 This gives you times and readouts between two GPS points.

The gearchange, for instance, is a masterwork in solid fluidity, with not a trace of excess movement in its short action. The driving position is perfect, the large wheel placed just where you want it. And then there's the engine out the back, that mighty 480bhp twin-turbo straight six, utterly unburstable and awesome in its power, slamming the car forward with indomitable force, all four wheels clawing the road. The 911 Turbo is still a player, vast in its all-round ability, docile when it needs to be, fast as well.

But driving these two cars back-to-back, it's not long before you realise that the Nissan makes it seem old-fashioned. The GT-R's balance and body control is extraordinary through faster, bumpy bends that will have the 911 unsettled enough to have the driver lose confidence – not only a good driver, but a fairly regular enthusiast driver like myself. I had a number of heart-in-mouth moments in the Turbo trying to keep up with the GT-R, even with the Porsche's suspension set to its harder 'sport' setting. It still seems soft, and there's a bouncy lack of balance in the way the suspension controls the body, and the way the big engine slung out the back threatens to swing round. By contrast, I never felt anything but natural solidity in the Nissan, adjustable and fluid.

The GT-R turns in beautifully, whether neutral or under brakes, and grips forever – slippery surfaces seem to bring out the best in it. Time after time I left Turner behind as my four-wheel-drive system and traction control worked better out of wet corners – it wasn't just the fact that I could get on the power earlier. It was about confidence. The Nissan really is something special, and you get the impression that while a master driver could wring every last ounce of performance out of the 911, your mother could do the same in the GT-R. And all the while, making lightning fast up- and down-changes in milliseconds while the Porsche driver messes with manual.

Does the Nissan's ability reduce the driving pleasure? Not at all. You can turn all the systems off if you so choose, and it's still supremely well balanced, no doubt a delight for a racing driver on a track. It doesn't feel as heavy as it is – it weighs a chunky 1740kg, 80kg more than the Porsche. But its supreme Nürburgring lap time of 7:38, a full two seconds faster than the Turbo (and on a partly wet track), is solely down to its completely planted feel, its awesome grip and traction, and the natural way it goes about maintaining speed through corners.

It feels high, almost on tip-toe in comparison to the 911, but that's because it is. It's a big car. But it's ⋮

Paddles edged in leather, attached to steering column rather than wheel

Driving these two cars back-to-back, it's not long before you realise that the Nissan makes the Porsche seem old-fashioned. The GT-R is truly extraordinary

For all-round ability, I have no doubt the Niss is the best car I have ever driven. It's a solid car you can rely on when the going gets trick

not slow. Our 'bahn tests proved that. From medium revs in fourth gear, with me driving the Nissan and with a passenger on board, the radio count-down allowed us to nail the throttles simultaneously with the cars side-by-side. Turner's Porsche crawled forward, and I mean crawled, v-e-r-y slowly. It only highlights the supernatural performance of the GT-R.

For all-round ability, I have no doubt the Nissan is the best car I've ever driven. It is almost as fast as the Porsche – which means it's almost as fast as any car on earth – and inspires more confidence through corners, yet it's also more roomy and practical and has a proper modern gearbox. It's a big, solid car you can rely on when the going gets tricky, that you can

thrash around a track, then set the suspension to soft, the transmission to auto, the Bose audio to full bass and potter into town without a trace of angst.

Oh, I nearly forgot – price. The 911 Turbo comes in at about £100,000, which is good value for such a stupendous car, but the GT-R will cost about £40,000 less than that when it goes on sale in the UK in 2009. Mizuno-san is right. This car has no competitors. Not at any price. But that won't prevent one of the first GT-Rs in Europe being bought by an anonymous man and taken to Porsche AG in Stuttgart for a thorough examination. With an even more powerful and lighter V Spec GT-R on the way, Porsche can't afford to lag behind for long.

EDGE OF REASON

The Dodge Viper ACR takes no prisoners with its insane 8.4-litre V10 that puts 600bhp on the tarmac. Pat Devereux gets to grips with an American psycho

Photography by Anton Watts

THERE'S A WAR GOING ON IN THE US right now. It's got nothing to do with bombs and guns – but everything to do with firepower.

While all the US carmakers are rushing to get small, economical cars onto their dealer lots as oil prices spurt to over $100 a barrel and house prices plunge from their all-time highs, two of them are still locked in mortal combat to produce the most heinous, fire-breathing production car on the planet.

In the blue corner we have GM's 2009 Chevrolet Corvette ZR1: This range-topping supercharged 6.2-litre missile bristles with carbon fibre – bonnet and roof are now all the woven black stuff – and has a top speed only a Bugatti could beat. It's so fast they've had to rework the speedo so it now reads up to 220mph instead of the standard car's 200.

In the red corner, the ACR Viper. Good enough to beat the ZR1?

Boasting more power than NATO and more torque than the Women's Institute, the ZR1, codenamed Blue Devil, also threatens to pull your face off in the corners by generating almost as much sideways gravity as a fighter jet. You'll be able to see exactly how much on the *Top Gun*-style head-up display – when you're not blacking out from the acceleration.

It's got plenty of other trick bits, too. A bigger, stronger clutch so you can do bigger, longer burnouts. A six-speed close-ratio gearbox instead of the standard car's arm-length throw, and carbon ceramic brakes, just like the Corvette Le Mans cars. It even has suspension you can adjust to track-level stiffness from the comfort of your heavily bolstered seat.

So, it seems fair to say, it's going to be a fearsome weapon when it arrives in late 2008. Skylines, Ferraris, Lamborghinis...nothing will be safe when the $100,000 ZR1 hits the streets running. Least of all the poor old Viper, you'd think.

How on earth could the big Dodge beat the ZR1's *Star Wars* spec sheet? I mean, it's great fun smoking the tyres on the big Viper but it's hardly a 21st century device is it? It's still got a steel chassis and it hasn't got any carbon fibre anywhere, for heaven's sake. It's about as modern as a battering ram.

Well, OK, it's not the cutting edge, but the red corner has added a couple of new tricks – and, yes, some carbon fibre – to the Viper playbook. And it's confident its new $98,000 car, the ACR, can still take the fight to the new 'Vette. It's not quite ∴

The Viper is hardly a 21st century device. It's still got a steel chassis, for heaven's sake. It's as modern as a battering ram

Horizontal beats vertical, width beats height, wing beats airstream

Pat's a hooligan and we approve massively. Don't go changin', y'hear

Designed to be the kind of car you can drive to the track, thrash around, then drive home, the ACR turns the Viper into a racer for the road

You wouldn't think those sunbursts are deliberate, but they are. Clever

pitchforks versus lasers as, for all its trick techno bits, the ZR1 is still also a big, pushrod-engined car at heart. But it's not far off.

So why do the Dodge people seem so confident? Well, for a start, despite the Corvette's Le Mans success and apparent technological lead, in Z06 form, the Viper SRT-10 is the faster, better handling car. In all comparison tests, the Viper has covered the quarter mile, the dash to 60mph and cornered faster than the 'Vette Z06 could manage. That's why.

The how is a little more technical, but not much. The Viper is wider, lower, longer and, despite appearances, has a seven-inch shorter wheelbase than the 'Vette. The big Dodge might tip the scales a couple of hundred pounds heavier than the Chevy, but then its engine is a battle-ready 8.4-litre V10 that fires 600hp to the rear wheels. The Corvette Z06 has to make do with a relatively weedy 7.0-litre V8 that can muster a mere 505hp to torture the rear tyres.

That's in standard form. In ZR1 spec, the 'Vette trumps the Viper's power by a comfortable margin. So that should make it quickest through the quarter and in a straight line. And the new suspension should shave a few tenths off its lap times, so maybe it'll get a little closer in the corners, too.

But now that Dodge has fired back with the ACR – that's short for American Club Racer – maybe it won't. The new Viper's engine remains as stock, so the big 'Vette might win the straightline battle, but it's doubtful it'll win the lap-time war because this Viper ACR, the third since 1999, is packing some serious handling heat under its bodyshell.

As Chief Viper Development Engineer, Herb Helbig, said when he showed us around the prototype ACR: "It's going to take a bit more than just putting a supercharger on the Corvette to make it beat this." As we're going to discover, he's not wrong.

Designed to be the kind of car you can drive to the track, thrash against your mates, then drive home again, the ACR turns the already uncompromising Viper into a just-add-numbers racer for the road. It's lighter, better handling, faster stopping and more outrageous than it's ever been before. Perfect.

It weighs in 40lb – half a tank of petrol – lighter than the standard car, thanks to lighter tyres, wheels and brakes. But it can shed another 40lb with the optional Hard Core package in place. That deletes the audio system, underbonnet sound-proofing, boot carpet and tyre inflator, replacing them with a lap timer and some carbon-fibre panels. It also brings the weight of the car to within an ace of the weight of the ZR1, cancelling out the 'Vette's bulk advantage.

But, rather than making the ACR's top speed higher, the rest of its new bits are designed to make the car quicker around a track than along the drag strip. Instead of messing with the engine, which they reasoned makes more than enough power, the Street and Racing Technology team worked on improving the Viper's grip, to make more of the power useable more of the time. This involved night after night in the windtunnel – after the Dodge NASCAR team had finished with it – subtly reworking the Viper's shape to increase its downforce.

Rather like the Ferrari Scuderia, the final shape they emerged with isn't that much different from the standard car's form, but the differences to the car's performance are significant.

Where the standard Viper generates about 100lb of downforce at 150mph (which is better than the majority of big sports cars – most generate lift at speed) the ACR makes 1,000lb of downforce at the same speed. What that means is that, when the car hits naughty motorway speeds, an invisible baby elephant appears on the roof of the car and squashes it into the road.

This allows the Viper to corner at previously unthinkable, spin-off-and-die speeds. Even though the team were still doing final tests on the aero kit, which involves an adjustable depth front 'fanged' splitter, a good sized rear spoiler and all manner of bodywork tweaks, they reckoned they were seeing around 1.5g of lateral, lunch-loosening g in fast corners.

What allowed them to come back and tell us that fact is the new suspension. Supplied by KW Suspensions and tuned specifically for track performance, the ACR's set-up is adjustable for damping and ride height without removing the wheels. It's a long way from the convenience of the Corvette's push-button system, but then it's a lot more serious, too.

The brakes are remarkably similar, though. Both have huge carbon ceramic brakes that are almost the same size as the wheels, and calipers the size of toasters. So you can expect similar, freeze-frame style, get-your-eyeballs-off-my-windscreen braking performance from the pair of them.

Well, I say you can expect it for both of them. While we are going to have to find out later how the ZR1 drives, I'm going to know about the ACR in less than one minute as I've just heard the car bellow noisily into life in the garage behind me. That means it's my turn to thrash it – there is only one car, so no pressure – around the track here at Willow Springs in the high desert above LA.

As I pull on my gloves, the clear blue sky suddenly darkens, the wind picks up and I feel a few drops of rain on my face. Oh great. I look at the ACR's cut-slick Michelin Pilot Sport Cup tyres, remember the 600bhp output and swallow hard. The invite said to bring a fire suit and helmet. But I didn't get the invite, so I turned up in jeans and sunglasses. Hmmm.

No time for second thoughts now, though. Strapped into the car in a four-point racing harness, all the trademark Viper cues are there. Cramped cabin, check. Just see over the steering wheel, check. Earthquake exhaust note, check. Heart rate over 150bpm, check...

As I fiddle nervously with the few controls that are left in the cabin after the Hard Core boys have done their deleting, Herb Helbig leans in through the netting window, pulls the cigar from his mouth and shouts at me: "Just remember that the tyres are cold. And watch the wind out of turn eight.

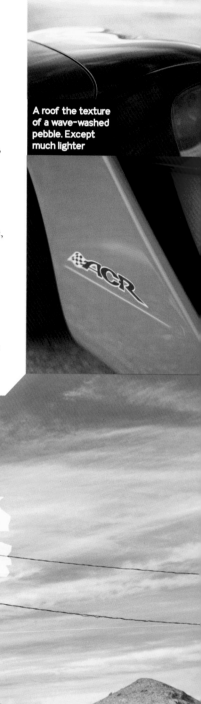

A roof the texture of a wave-washed pebble. Except much lighter

Where the standard Viper generates about 100lb of downforce at 150mph, the ACR makes 1,000lb

An 8.0-litre V10 takes some cooling. Hence the many, many vents

You big fat mutha, you're all curves and beefiness you are. Ooh, ooooh!

All aero details honed by the wizards in the Dodge NASCAR wind tunnel

These little lips are doing something. Even if they don't, they'd look cool

Put a wheel off the track there, and your drive is over. D'ya hear?"

Cold. Wind. Off. Over. I nod responsibly, then jam it into first and blast off down to turn one, like you do when you're in a 600bhp race car. But like you probably shouldn't in a 3,300lb Viper on cold tyres on a track you've only seen recently on a couple of sighting laps in a van at 40mph.

Before I go any further, I should explain that a Viper has the laziest power delivery this side of a water wheel. As the road speed soars, the engine note hardly changes. Add to this the wide-spaced gears, two of which are largely unnecessary due to the endless amount of torque and, despite its ferocious appearance, it is a strangely relaxing car to drive fast.

Which is my excuse for why I've just arrived at this first left hander 30mph quicker than I probably should have. I think about panicking but there isn't time, so I just hit the brakes, slip it down a gear – more to use the new slick shifter than for any need – throw it in and get back on the gas.
The ACR is not in the slightest bit bothered.

So I do it again in turn two, a double apex right, and the Viper just sticks and goes. Turn three, a tight uphill left hander that flicks right at the top of a small hill into turn four. It would be a challenge for any car to keep itself together through this, particularly a big fella like this Viper. But it's not even vaguely upset by it. Turn five, easy. Turn six, a blind crest onto the back straight, not an issue. Turn seven, really just a kink, like it's not even there.

But then comes turn eight. This has to be one of the fastest corners on any non-oval track in the US. A tightening radius right, I've driven a couple of cars around here that have tied themselves in knots – along with my guts – trying to get though and out of it cleanly. If anything was going to go wrong in the ACR, this was going to be the place.

Needn't have worried. Even hopelessly off-line, the Viper can be adjusted with all the ease of something half its size. It's not quite as easy as an Elise, but it's several miles better than anything else of this size and power. The steering is meaty and direct. The grip is astonishing and it never seems to lose its composure. Oh, and it's very, very fast.

The whole experience was completely different to how I had imagined it would be. Rather than having to rough handle some wheezing old nail around the track, the ACR was fast, smooth and amazingly sure-footed.

Which is the type of car even quite inexperienced petrolheads could buy, drive to the track, race without crashing, then drive home again. And, as that's exactly what Dodge tried to build with this car, it looks like it's made a direct hit.

We know the alloy-framed ZR1 is going to be good on the road, and will probably win that battle against the ACR. It wouldn't be that hard after all. But having driven this big new Viper, I'd say the new 'Vette better have something very special up its wheelarches or this is one war, on the track at least, it could very easily lose.

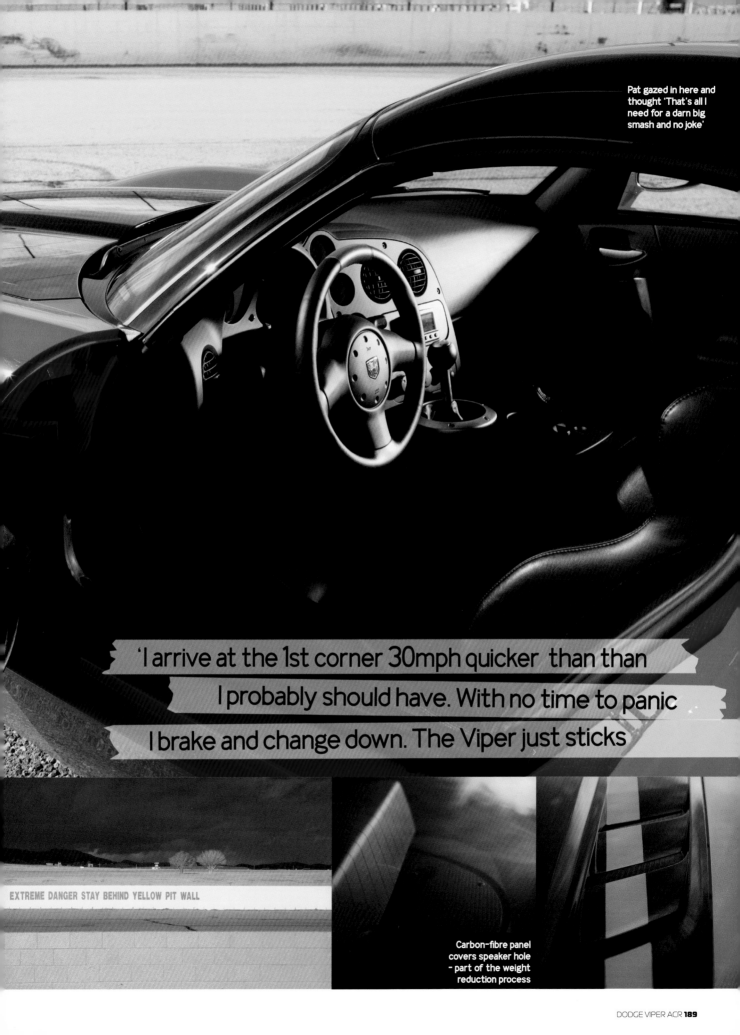

Pat gazed in here and thought 'That's all I need for a darn big smash and no joke'

'I arrive at the 1st corner 30mph quicker than than I probably should have. With no time to panic I brake and change down. The Viper just sticks

EXTREME DANGER STAY BEHIND YELLOW PIT WALL

Carbon-fibre panel covers speaker hole - part of the weight reduction process

Take 1,793bhp care of the Koenigsegg CCX and Bugatti Veyron,
a stretch of deserted Arabian tarmac and one hard-boiled Stig.
Then stand well back, as the battle of the über cars begins

Desert

storm

Story by Bill Thomas Photography by Lee Brimble

HOW DO YOU COMPARE THE GREATEST supercars in the world? You do it properly, that's how. You take them to the best driving road you can think of, you give them the time and the space to run at speed, you get the road closed by the cops to eliminate risk to the public, and then you hope The Stig turns up.

He did, of course, seemingly unaffected by the 45° heat, striding across the desert from the direction of Ayn al-Faydah toward the base of the Jebel Hafeet mountain. This 4,068ft-high limestone alp is one of the most spectacular places in the Arabian Gulf, rising straight up from the plains above the city of Al Ain, two hours east of Abu Dhabi, capital of the United Arab Emirates. The views on the way up are incredible, and it's an amazing-looking geological wonder, but forget all that – the multi-lane road cutting its way up to the summit is new and beautifully surfaced, the corners majestic and challenging and varying in radius and severity. If there is a road more suited to The Stig, I can't think of it. Let's go.

ETIHAD FLIGHT 8 LANDED ON TIME AT 7:20AM after its 3,000-mile flight from Frankfurt. As the passengers filed off the aircraft and into the arrivals hall at Abu Dhabi airport, none of them could have guessed what was lurking beneath the

floor of their Airbus A340... a bright red Koenigsegg CCX, £450,000-worth of Swedish supercar. Etihad kindly flew it in for us (see panel) because none of the four Koenigseggs in the Gulf was available. Soon it was burbling out of the airport, on its way directly to Al Ain and a meeting with the supercar ruler of the Middle East – and everywhere else – the Bugatti Veyron.

If we take the American Shelby SSC Ultimate Aero out of the picture – production of that car isn't underway yet – the Veyron and CCX are the fastest cars in the world. Koenigsegg claims to have run a CCX-R at 260mph in private testing, while the £683,000 Veyron's official maximum is 253mph. The Koenigsegg has 'only' 806bhp compared to the Veyron's 987bhp, but it's worth noting that the Swedish car is considerably lighter, 1,473kg plays 1,888kg, and slipperier too. The Koenigsegg holds no fear of its German rival.

It was a matter of letting Stig drive first, and working my pitiful efforts around him. The Veyron, the only all-white example in the world, was provided by a private owner (see Bug Club, following this feature), because Bugatti will not sanction or support any comparison involving one of its cars. That's a stupid attitude to take, but there it is. Stig didn't seem to care. He'll just drive whatever's given to him.

Off he went into the heat, swapping back and forth, disappearing for random periods, then swapping again, striding across from one car to the other without a micron of wasted energy. The sheer walls of Jebel Hafeet echoed to the sounds of a twin-supercharged V8 and a quad-turbo W16, accompanied by the occasional whoosh and chirrup of tyres. Never a screeching howl, nothing lurid. Just hard, precise, fast piloting. The Stig avoided any incidents with the Koenigsegg – he has a history with this car, as we know... try YouTubing it – but still quite clearly took it right to the very limit. He was on it. After a full 40 minutes, Stigster seemed satisfied. He walked off in the direction of Al Maqam.

My turn, then. I wish Stig could write – it would save me a lot of time. But it's no hardship telling you about these extraordinary cars.

First, the Veyron. You may have read about it before, you may have seen it on the telly racing across Europe and taking on Eurofighters. But none of that can really prepare you for the shock of the acceleration when you open the throttle and unleash nearly 1,000bhp and 923lb ft of torque. It will get to 100mph in 5.5 seconds and 0–150mph in 9.8 seconds. That's about the same time it takes a Lexus IS-F to get to 100. Lunacy. The Bugatti is immensely fast, with its fury ⠿

380mm diameter discs, just so you know

I'll take a ride in either one, thanks, not fussy

Stig poses in wrong seat for reasons to do with art. He's not happy about it, either

Touch the bottom three switches of the circle in the right order, and she starts

'The Stig managed to avoid any incidents with the Koenigsegg – he has a history with this car as we know... But he still quite clearly took it right to the limit'

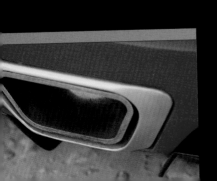

KOENIGSEGG CCX
Price £636,886
Capacity 4700cc
Bhp 806bhp
Torque 693lb ft
Weight 1473kg
0-62mph 3.2secs
Top speed 245mph+

Koenigsegg interior is simple and fuss-free. With just a hint of 'brothel-chic' to it

CCX

Calm, peaceful desert sunset, beautiful light, and a £683,000 car

Ǝ3B

70316 A.D.

'I understood why so many Veyron owners also have a Koenigsegg – they have an all-rounder in the Veyron and a racer in the Koenigsegg'

Bugatti interior is a masterwork of retro design. With just a hint of 'brothel-chic' to it

BUGATTI VEYRON
Price £785,158
Capacity 7933cc
Bhp 987bhp
Torque 923lb ft
Weight 1,888kg
0–62mph 2.5secs
Top speed 253mph+

delivered in a huge surge of turbo boost. This 8.0-litre W16 engine would deliver amazing performance without the four turbochargers. But they're there. Cool.

Slicing up the Jebel Hafeet road, snicking through the supremely fast and effective paddle-shift sequential gearbox, it was immediately obvious that there's a lot more to this car than straight-line grunt. Its four-wheel-drive chassis gives it massive traction out of corners, though the traction control light blinks in an instant if you're lead-footed. More impressive is the way it changes direction – you get quite a lot of feel for what the tyres are doing, and the overwhelming sensation is one of 'plantedness', a solidity drawn from many thousands of hours of testing and money-no-object engineering by masters. The steering's a bit dead in a Mercedes kind of way, but the weighting is fine. It's wonderfully quiet and refined too, the Veyron. There's a big sense of engine from behind your head, but it's never overly loud or intrusive. You could travel many hundreds of miles in this thing and remain comfortable, as did Jeremy when he raced James's plane across Europe.

The Koenigsegg is a different type of animal altogether, and in a few seconds I understood why so many Koenigsegg owners also have a Veyron. It's the perfect combination – an all-rounder in the Veyron, a racer in the Koenigsegg.

It's raw, this Swedish thing – aggressive, loud to the point of ear damage when it revs, and very much a track car in its unforgiving, direct nature. I mentioned loud, did I? And it is, very loud. But why shouldn't it be? This is a supercar, not a shopping trolley, and it's not as if that 4.7-litre twin-supercharged V8 sounds nasty. It sounds wonderful, without the wearing supercharger whine you usually get from such engines. It's a simple V8 yell.

Put your foot on the throttle violently, and the whole car snaps forward in an instant, bang. Do the same in the Veyron, and the computer will have a very quick think about it, the turbos will come on boost and you'll then be accelerated into the next dimension. That whole process takes no time at all, but you notice it, and the throttle pedal is very slightly fuzzy. The Koenigsegg's throttle pedal, by contrast, is like a delicate, sharp, snapping switch, one that you can adjust to very small degress if you need to. This is a pure driver's car.

Even more impressive is the way the car rides. It's magic. I found some hacked-up sections at the bottom of the mountain, and the Swede really glided over them. It is far from uncomfortable – it is a beautifully engineered machine, and its subtlety genuinely surprised me.

Most of all though, it's immensely fast. The engine noise is ridiculous... and the speed, well, Jesus. A recent 0–300km/h–0 test carried out by

a German magazine clocked this CCX at 29.2secs. No Veyron was present – Bugatti doesn't help with such things, remember – so the next fastest car was the McLaren SLR 722. It was line-ball between it and the Koenigsegg from 0 to 200km/h (120mph), but then the Swedish beast was 6.5 seconds faster from 200 to 300km/h (186mph). That's a lot, and it says everything about the car's immense performance.

It's probably still not quite as fast as a Veyron, but it's not far off. More important than the pure speed is the way the CCX feels to drive – perfectly weighted steering, an extremely nimble, light-weight feel to the chassis through corners, and that magic ride quality. It really is a brilliant piece of work – one that shouldn't be underestimated. I think you'll find we'll be driving it again soon.

So which car wins this face-off to end all face-offs? Ultimately, it's the Veyron, because it is probably the greatest engineering feat in automotive history. It's inefficient, yes, and it's far from green, but, by God, it's fast, and it combines that monumental speed with real luxury inside, and a quiet, relaxed cockpit ambience when you're not in a hurry. If you happen to see a Koenigsegg drive by when you're in your Bugatti, you'll know that its driver is having more fun, a more exciting experience, but you simply won't care. Because if you wanted to, you could have him. Because the Veyron rules. And probably always will. TG

No messing in here – it's pure decadence

Turn the speed key, and wing/airbrake is deployed

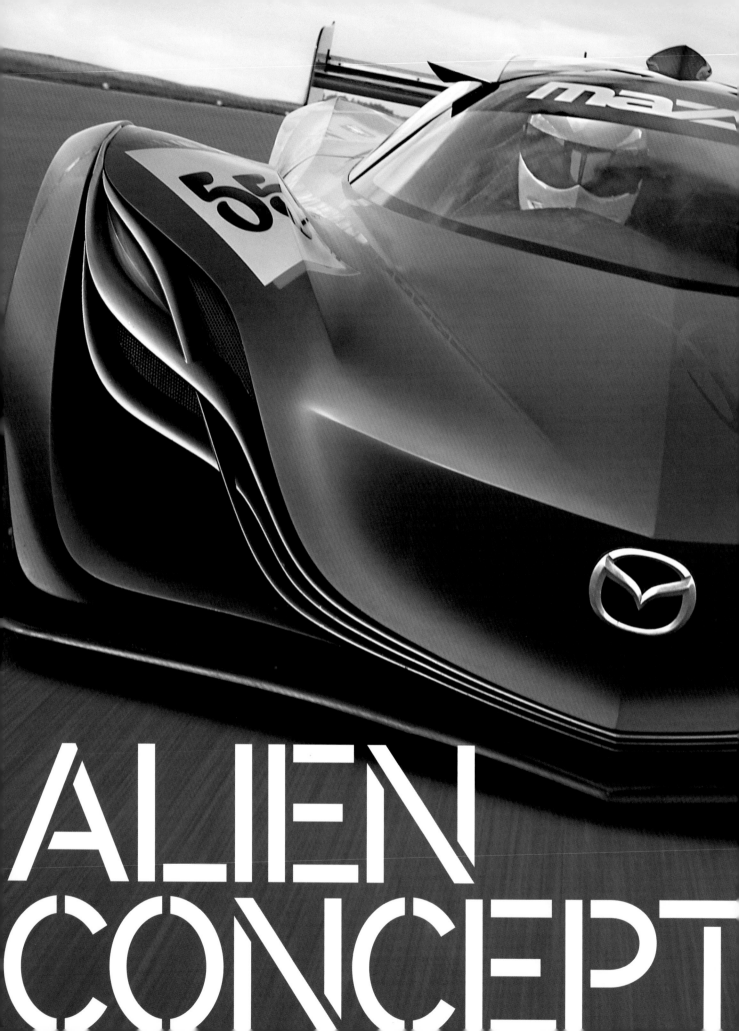

ALIEN CONCEPT

Photography Lee Brimble

Could it be that the Mazda Furai and The Stig hail from the same planet? **Bill Thomas** has a close encounter with both of them on a deserted runway

LOOK AT THE CAR ON THIS PAGE AND THEN look at what's driving it. Do you think The Stig would show any sort of interest in concept cars normally? I'll give you a clue: the answer is 'no'. Concept cars are usually created as design exercises for motorshows, pure showpieces to display how future styling might look for whatever marque is concerned, things that sit on rotundas under glittering lights and rotate for the interest of passers-by. Concept cars are not Stig fare. They can be wild creations that have no relationship with reality whatever, let alone anything that might run. Concept cars – usually – weigh about 58 tons because they're built on ridiculous chassis that don't have to be light or even roll or steer, and sometimes their bodywork is made of clay. Power comes from a battery pack to keep the lights on, not an engine, and the interior is usually completely non-functional too. Pure design doesn't have to be useful.

Mazda has been as active as any manufacturer in the world with its concept cars. The five most recent have followed a similar theme, which the Mazda styling team calls 'Nagare'. The first Nagare concept was called 'Nagare'. Then there was the Ryuga, Hakaze and Taiki. The last of these, the Taiki, was the maddest, with outrider wheels at the back. Google them for a good look and know, deep down in your soul, that while they might be wonderful pieces of design, The Stig has never Googled these puppies. Assuming he ever Googles anything, which is unlikely.

But the Furai you see here is different, and makes up for every scrap of non-functionality paraded by the previous four Nagare non-runner thingamees, obliterates their complete uselessness in one very high-pitched rotary bark. Because the Furai is not only the wildest-looking car in all creation, it also happens to be a bloody serious racing car underneath. A 460bhp rotary-engined Courage C65 Le Mans Prototype (LMP2) racer, no less, running on

'How cool is this? An airgun is jabbed into one of the wheelhubs. Not what you expect of a design study'

E100 ethanol. And today, we're going to be the only magazine in the world to drive it.

We're at Bentwaters Parks, a former RAF base beyond nowhere on the wrong side of Ipswich. The wind is blowing across this bleak outpost in a fashion that only British airfields can serve up wind; constant and strong and brisk and cutting. Apt that 'Furai' means 'sound of wind', then. The sound is constant, and soon there'll be some more urgent sounds accompanying it. Please prepare your computer if it's handy. This story works better with some web accompaniment.

We're out on the main runway, which is nearly two miles long, and a truck has arrived. It stops nearby, we say our greetings to the occupants, Mazda's engineering crew from America, and then a concept car is wheeled out the back of it. From now on, I'm not going to fully respect any concept car that isn't wheeled out of the back of a truck at an airfield. And I'm not going to respect any concept car that doesn't have its own air jack system.

Have a look at the main photo on this page. How cool is this? A man is jamming an airgun onto one of this concept car's wheelhubs. Again, not the sort of thing you normally associate with a design study. Look at those fantastic sweeping lines running up and around the headlight, look at the headlight's shape, look at the alloy blade mirrors on top of the doors, look at the way the body is sculpted between the beautiful wheel arches. Computational Fluid Dynamics (CFD, the technique favoured by money-no-object F1 teams) was used to help sculpt this shape and make it aerodynamically efficient. It is – those wings aren't there for show – and it's also mildly frightening. What a thing.

So, any nerves before driving a priceless one-off concept, then? Nope. None at all. I conquered my nerves forever by

driving Sebastian Bourdais' 800bhp Champ Car for an issue of Top Gear magazine and that cured my nerves. But the fact that I drove that car meant I was allowed to have a shot in this one. Mazda insisted that you had to have experience in a racing car of similar power, with a similar gearbox.

The car's systems were primed and it was fired up. It ticked over with a machine-gun staccato hammer, like some sort of super-scooter – bap-bap-bap-bap-bap. The engine is a normally-aspirated 13B/20B triple-rotor job, as used by some teams in the American Le Mans series. It had only just come back from the United States following a blow-up on a previous drive day in the UK. The engine had never run in the car in its current form, but it sounded healthy enough as it ticked over with its constant patter.

Mazda works driver Mark Ticehurst took the wheel first to do a shakedown and make sure all systems were normal. He climbed aboard and gunned it up the runway. What an utterly fabulous engine note! Hear it for yourself if you haven't already – Youtube search 'Mazda Furai' and watch it in action at Laguna Seca in California. And, perhaps more importantly, drink in that engine sound. One of my favourite bits in that video happens at 3min 12sec, when the car lowers itself onto the ground. But my absolutely favourite bit happens at 4:38. Watch that thing accelerate away and listen to it wail!

I digress. And I'm going to digress a bit more. My humble apologies if you don't have access to the internet right now, but please do one more Youtube search if you do: 'Mazda Furai Concept extended with sound'. Look and listen to that one. Hear that buzzing, high-pitched, stabbing staccato riff, that laughing, demented goat sound, like a giant bee has mated with a buzz-saw? That's what the Furai sounds like at tickover. Then turn up the volume and listen to it ripping past. Zaaar!! ⋮

The Stig sees to it that Mazda have to make a wheel change or two

Precision steering with a 'wheel not much bigger than a beer mat

"When it starts to scream like a demonic goat, change up a gear"

Off Ticehurst went, making that very sound. Then he came back and reported a vibration at the rear end. Wheels were changed and he went up again. All's fine, engine running smoothly, no leaks. It looked fast, very fast, and it left a gigantic rooster tail of dust in its wake as it tore back and forth. There were so many non-concept car things happening here all in quick succession it was difficult to keep track of them. And every time the thing pushed itself off the road with its air jacks, I became more convinced that this is the coolest car in the world. Given the enormous publicity it's generated, I couldn't stop myself hoping that other manufacturers might start creating concept cars like this.

After a run in the passenger seat with Mark driving, it was time to slot behind the wheel. The front-hinged beetle-wing doors allow good access, but you still have to clamber over wide sculpted sills, coloured red and grey with flowing ridges, which I was hesitant to lean on.

"You can put your weight on anything," said engineer Marcus Haselgrove. This really is a proper racing car, then. And it was at that moment that The Stig appeared, jerked a thumb at me in a fashion that wasn't hard to understand, and promptly belted himself in and took off. It's beyond me how Stig finds out about these things, but there he was, taking to the taxiways and finding corners wherever he could. He wasn't in the car for long, but it needed more ethanol by the time he was finished. The Furai zoomed back towards our position and Stig cut the engine early as it rolled to a halt with a lonely zim of whine from the gearbox. The car smelt of brake discs and heat. Stig then walked off in the direction of Campsey Ash. His first concept car drive seemed to go quite well.

Finally, my turn. I wouldn't be driving it like The Stig did, but I could get an idea. Once you slide down into the cockpit it's actually quite comfortable. The tiny racing wheel is right in your chest, and the rest of the cockpit is beautifully designed and detailed. There are no instruments on the dash – all of the information you need is provided by the LCD screen on the steering wheel, which has various modes selectable by the buttons on either side of it. Change-up lights stretch across the top of its rim. They light up from either side, and when the blue central ones are all lit, it's time to change up using the right-hand paddle, the paddles being where you'd expect, on the wheel. ⁞

'Your helmet is pushed back into the headrest. You know you're aboard something properly fast'

A work of art in themselves, the Furai's alloys are spectacular

'The final step needs to be taken and I won't rest until it is – this car needs to race. At Le Mans'

The movement of the paddles themselves is tiny, precise and military-grade in its action. Little short of perfection.

With Ticehurst strapped in alongside to keep a watching brief on my muppetry, I fired her up – punch fuel and ignition switches on the roof first, then hit the rotary-shaped starter button in the centre of the dash. The little engine sounds remote from the cockpit and is no louder at tickover than a fast road car, at least when you're wearing a helmet. There wasn't much shoulder room with Ticehurst sitting there in the passenger seat, but solo, you'd be comfortable here for as long as it took – a two hour stint at Le Mans wouldn't be a problem.

Clutch is short but easy. We're moving. The engine just wants to go, it doesn't like this low-speed manouevering, it wants to be revving. Hmm. It's well warmed up after Stig's run, everything's ready to rock, we're at low to middling revs in first gear in a straight line on a dry surface, may as well push the throttle all the way to the firewall and see what happens.

It goes. Hard. As you'd expect with a rotary engine, revs build mighty quickly. Those little steering wheel lights are blinking at you a lot sooner than you expect. Click the right paddle. Whack. The next gear is engaged in a zillisecond with a forceful thump. There is no discernable let-up in acceleration in second, third or fourth. Your helmet is pushed back into the headrest and you know you're aboard something properly fast. And it feels fast, despite the open expanses of Bill-friendly runway. It's only when you get the Furai into fifth gear that you start to feel the aero pushing the car down and the drag from that gigantic rear wing starting to make itself felt.

We topped out at about 160mph in sixth before I backed off. It's geared to do about 185mph. The brakes are stupendous and the downshift as smooth as silk when you're braking hard, blipping the engine with dramatic forcefulness – under gentle braking, this manic blipping actually pushes the car forward. Round we go in a giant U-turn at the end of the runway – the steering wheel is

small but a joy to use, its movement tiny, only one turn lock-to-lock, but it's all very straightforward and natural to drive. And hugely rewarding. After a few runs I'd completely forgotten I was driving a concept car. This is a well-sorted race car with an exceptionally light and powerful and responsive engine. It doesn't rev as high as you'd think, peaking at 8,800rpm, but it sounds like it's revving to about 15,000. Peak torque is only 278lb ft, again at 8,800rpm! But it's all perfectly smooth and precise, the kind of racing car that would reward delicacy and accuracy rather than brute force.

Time to develop some lateral G, and the Furai is even more impressive now, hurling us left and right as I weave on the straight at high speed. No body-roll, huge grip, phenomenal cornering power with downforce very much providing the godlike downward shove to make it possible. Again, time for a reality check – this is an other-worldy concept car, a design exercise, a work of high automotive art, and we're pulling at least 3G in these corners!

Mazda deserves a medal for building this wonderful machine. It's an inspired piece of work, probably the greatest concept car ever produced. Certainly the most visually striking. It was built to enhance Mazda's motorsport image, especially in America, where more Mazdas are raced at club level than any other type of car. But I'm sorry, it's not quite enough. The final step needs to be taken and I don't think I'll rest until it is – this car needs to race. At Le Mans. To see a brace of Furai's, front strips glowing between piercing headlights, brake discs burning into Indianapolis, airscoops lifted into the wind stream, dicing with lesser cars, rolling into the pits for driver changes and fuel... That's what I'm talking about. I don't care whether they win or lose. I just want to see it.

Mazda's Chief Financial Officer in America is a bloke called David E. Friedman. Dave, this is a personal and direct message to you from *Top Gear,* an appeal from the heart. Sign off a few million. Get the Furai onto the track in anger. Please. Message ends. 🔳

Vat of plutonium added to get the monster up to warp speed

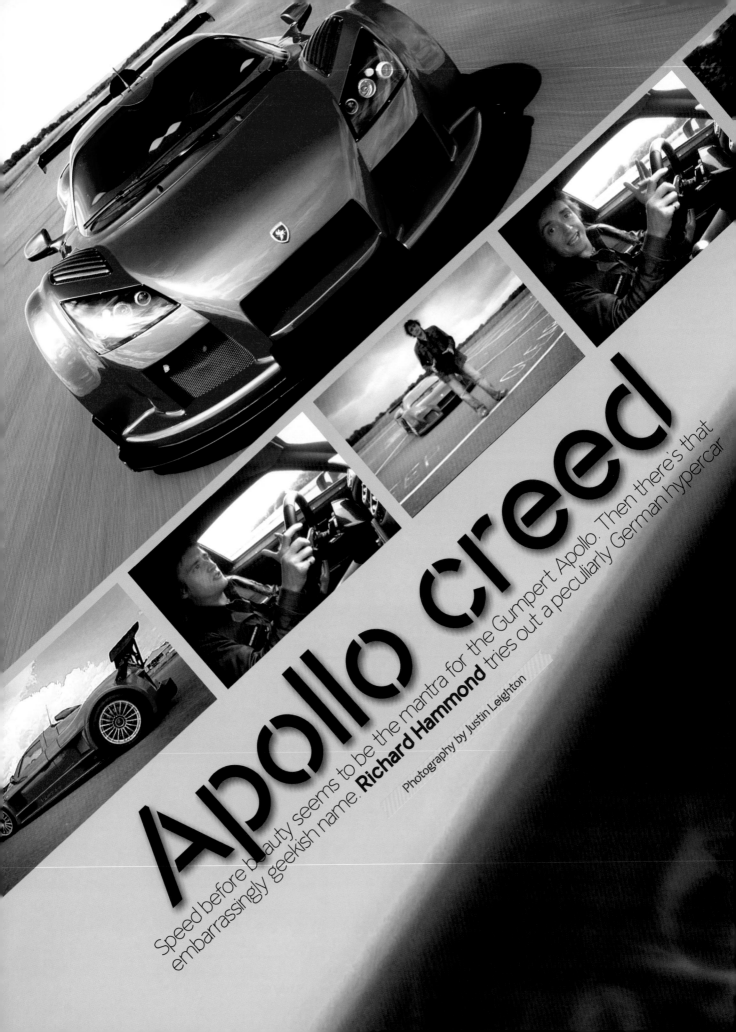

Apollo creed

Speed before beauty seems to be the mantra for the Gumpert Apollo. Then there's that embarrassingly geekish name. **Richard Hammond** tries out a peculiarly German hypercar

Photography by Justin Leighton

A WELL SLAPPED ARSE, A BULLDOG LICKING THE piss off a thistle, a melted wellie or a sightless moose after a dash through the ugly forest hitting every tree; take your pick. It's one of those, I'm pretty sure. Probaby the most revealing indictment of the Gumpert Apollo's, er, 'challenging' looks came when Clarkson revealed that he thought it looked good. Well there you go; a man who's had to stare at that jumbled bag of creases in the shaving mirror every morning for the last thousand years is, like someone wearing reverso-specs twenty four hours a day, eventually going to adapt and change the way he sees things.

Personally, I want the sight of a supercar – and boy, this is one if ever there was – to twang the heartstrings, quicken the breathing and give the trouser area a tweak for good measure. This one just made me feel a bit queasy and long for something nice to look at.

It is, obviously, a case of 'form following function' here. In other words, they can make it work, sure, but they can't make it pretty as well. But there's something deliberate and willfully obtuse about the pointy snout, the piggy eyes and the dumpy arse of the thing. Somehow, I can't imagine that it actually needs to be that ugly, just to be able to function. It's like London van-drivers who will actually go out of their way to inconvenience you – even if it takes more effort to pull across, change lanes and slow down to get in your way, they'll do it

Given his own name, The Stig has no problems with the Gumpert

Car's ugliness demands beer goggles. Drink-drive laws get in way

Everything inside is there for race purposes. It's all very serious

'There's something deliberate and willfully obtuse about the pointy snout, the piggy eyes and the dumpy arse. of the thing. Somehow. I can't imagine that it actually needs to be that ugly simply to function'

Tyres pre-Stig lap. Afterwards they were balder than a Kojak convention

just to piss you off and then claim it was because they needed to do it. And so, of course, the Apollo had better be pretty good to make up for it.

It is. You may have seen it hit the top of our leader board at the end of the series 11. It shot round the track in 1:17.1, making it faster than a Koenigsegg, a Porsche Carrera GT or a Zonda F. And it did it without seeming to get even slightly out of breath. And there's good reason for this; it's a race car that has been taught some nice manners so it can come into normal society without eating with its hands and pissing in the street. And as is often the way with these things, it's the brainchild of one bloke. He's one of those blokes driven by passion and fuelled by success, all that sort of stuff. These people have always been attracted to the motor industry for its excitement and its glitzy thrills. The bloke who turned round and saved Aston Martin through the 1980s, for instance, brought a combination of glamour, knowledge and confidence that the world found irresistible. He was called Victor Gauntlett, which is the coolest name anyone has ever had. This bloke is called Roland Gumpert. Which just isn't. And it explains why his car carries the legend 'Gumpert' on its badge and why even the model name, 'Apollo' can't quite lift the leaden weight of its family name.

But once again, it all boils down to what this thing can actually do. Roland used to be an engineer with Audi and has retained close links with the company. Which is, of course, a good thing. The Apollo uses a heavily-tweaked version of Audi's 4.2-litre V8 with a couple of turbochargers bunged on for good measure. Customers coughing up the £275,000 or so to buy one will have the choice of going for the full-power version, with 789bhp, the 690 bhp version or the beginner's

Hammond braces himself for raw acceleration to go with the raw looks

apollo S

Visual harmony, no. Uber-efficient weight distribution at all costs? Ja!

The Stig holds a walkie-talkie. He communicates using binary code

'This is clearly a GT racer, and its serious intent makes itself evident from the start. There are no stupid flappy paddles to operate the gearbox – it's a bloody great big lever'

model with a mere 649 bhp. But drivers won't get the choice of where to position the seat; it's fixed in place. The Gumpert's creators are, remember, German, and they came over very German when they got to the business of weight distribution. It's all well and good mounting the engine low and as close to the middle of the car as possible, and giving careful consideration to the position of the fuel tank, all in the name of keeping the car's balance as close to 50:50 as possible. But there's one great lump in there that just won't sit still and keeps on moving around: the driver. And so the engineers removed from this irritatingly weighty component the option of sliding the seat backwards and forwards and upsetting their perfect weight distribution. Instead, the seat is fixed in place and the steering wheel and pedals can slide backwards or forwards to accommodate the driver. I was nervous about lifting up my arms to grab the wheel in case it buggered it all up. But I did it anyway, belted the sequential 'box lever into first, lifted the heavyweight clutch pedal and took off.

And bloody hell did I ever take off. I don't know why they got so bothered about weight distribution. The Apollo hasn't really got any to distribute. And a lightweight car with 690bhp on tap (in this version) is never going to hang around. But that's just physics really, it's light, it's got a lot of power, it will go fast in a straight line. So would my desk.

The impressive stuff and the stuff that reveals just how much Roland Gumpert (can't help saying that name in a cod-Northern accent like I'm introducing him on stage at a Working Men's Club) knows about building cars, happens when you come to a corner. The suspension is fully adjustable and, assuming you haven't buggered it all up by re-setting stuff, is about as good as I've ever come across. You can feel the road surface through the seat, and through the steering wheel, bumps make their presence known because you need to know about them, you feel wheels beginning to lose their grip or finding it mid-corner because you need to know what they're doing. It is, in short, a much better car than I will ever be a driver.

This is clearly a GT racer, and its serious intent makes itself evident from the start. There are no stupid little plastic flappy paddles to operate the sequential gearbox, it's a bloody great big lever and you have to give it a proper belt to move between gears. The dash is well made and well trimmed, but it's only there to hold up the instruments telling you what the engine is doing. The only gimmick is a rear-view camera for reversing. And strictly speaking, that's not really a gimmick, it's there because there's no rear window.

The suspension and the physical gemoetry of the thing are what enable it to go so fast, not a load of computers nipping up wheels and distributing power where it can best do the job. It wants to go fast because that's what it was built to do.

The ride is good enough to cope with in daily life, away from the track, and it could probably cope with smaller lanes too. But why would you want to do that? It belongs, really, on the track; that's its home. It seems a shame to take it away from there. I love tigers, but I wouldn't want to keep one in my garden.

And the strangest things happened after a day with it. Once I really knew what it was about, what it was for and how good it was at doing it, I found that looking at it no longer made me feel physically sick. 🔳

VIRTUAL REALITY

What happens, asks **Matt Master**, when one of the world's most 'real' racing games gets into bed with a car maker wanting to prove its performance abilities?

Photography by Ripley and Ripley

CITROËN

IN THE VIRTUAL WORLD, ANYTHING goes. In the virtual world, it's OK to steal cars, bomb villages, gamble away a fortune, die, do it with hookers, die again. In the virtual world, you can ignore convention, practicality, morality, sanity and then just hit 'Restart'. What better place to design, build and race a car?

Small wonder, then, that Citroen, the company responsible for moments of divine madness like the 2CV and Maserati-engined DS, should have come up with the idea first. It's called the 'GTbyCitroen', by the way. And that's not a printing error. It really is just one word. 'Citroen GT' would have been way too easy. The 'GTbyCitroen' is a joint project between the French manufacturer and Polyphony Digital Inc, the company behind the astronomically successful *Gran Turismo* series of racing games. What we have here is a car intended solely for cyberspace, merely mimicked here for the stand at the Paris motor show.

The story starts with a chap called Takumi Yamamoto. He works for Citroen in France but is, we reckon, Japanese. So that's going to help. Now, apparently, he knows someone at Polyphony, and over a few late night *sakes*, these two hatched a plan. Takumi-san then approached Gilles Vidal, a Citroen employee with the entirely appropriate job title of Advanced Design Manager, and pitched the idea of a designing a virtual car for the next incarnation of *Gran Turismo*. Gilles was instantly on board. More pitches, more *sake*, and a final verdict was reached at Citroen HQ: "Allons-y..."

What with Peugeot going racing and building that TT-alike RC, and even Renault launching its Laguna Coupe, Citroen must have been feeling the pressure to, well, perform. Rallying prowess aside, there hasn't really been a sporty Citroen since they nailed up Jesus, and the *cachet* of such things is invaluable. One half-decent nod to high performance filters down in the buyer's psyche to the lowliest turd-box hatchback. That's why people like Honda and Renault persist in wasting billions in F1, why Peugeot went to Le Mans, and why Audi is still there kicking Peugeot's arse.

But those wasted billions are an issue. Campaigning a race car, or building a fast road car, is insanely expensive. So letting an employee draw one on his Mac that you then disseminate around the world via the most popular racing game in history is a stroke of penny-pinching genius.

And not only is it comparatively cheap, but it also allows you to go mental with the design. The GTbyCitroen (that's getting as tedious to write as it must be to read) is a very deliberate exercise in pure visual impact, with no regard for the limitations of real-world production. As Vidal explains: "We had a blank canvas, and the idea was to respect the racing ergonomics, but mix it together with something abstract. Almost like a sculpture." ∴

'THE GT BY CITROEN IS A DELIBERATE EXERCISE IN PURE VISUAL IMPACT, WITH NO REGARD FOR REAL-WORLD LIMITATIONS'

GT BY CITROEN IS THE SORT OF CAR THAT PEOPLE WOULD GET OUT OF THE WAY OF ON MOTORWAYS

SO, EXPLAIN TO ME AGAIN
WHY THIS ISN'T GOING
INTO PRODUCTION?

SWOOPING BODYWORK,
PRETTY LIGHTS, LOTS OF
MESH – MUST BE A CONCEPT

INSPIRATION CAME
DIRECTLY FROM *2001:
A SPACE ODYSSEY*

HURRAH, IT'S ABOUT
TIME WE HAD A GULL-
WING CAR IN THE MAG

WHEEL LOOKS A
LOT LIKE A COMPUTER-
GAME WHEEL.
COINCIDENCE?

CARBON-FIBRE WING
MIRRORS: EASY TO
REPAIR IF DAMAGED...

The car's design takes into account how *GT5* will be played too, with drivers being offered a variety of perspectives from which to drive and review their races. So every given angle on the car, and even the first-person interior view, has been thought through to create the most flattering appearance possible.

The car has been released as part of a *Gran Turismo 5 Prologue Spec III* bundle sold with the PlayStation 3 console. It is also available as a free download for *Prologue*, providing you're registered to the PlayStation 3 network. How the car will drive is vital. The *Gran Turismo* series has built its reputation on accurately replicating the way in which different cars will go, stop and handle, and this process was brought to bear on the GTbC, even though it doesn't exist. Citroen worked out how much power and torque its imaginary hydrogen fuel cell would generate, how it would be sprung, slowed, everything. And all this data was loaded into Polyphony's brain, and translated into virtual performance. And of course, when *GT5* comes out, you'll be able to drive it around the *Top Gear* track...

The clear advantage of this radical approach is that eventually we all get to drive it. And from Citroen's perspective, it's far closer to the designers' ideal of how their car should be perceived and enjoyed than your usual show car – normally bits of plastic and superglue with a lawnmower engine, if you're lucky.

But with a car as striking as this one, a car that is soon to be launched into the consciousness of the world's gaming millions, the superglue was bound to get used sooner or later. After all, Citroen needs to get its product seen, and to get people believing in the future of the brand.

So the vast, heavily sculptural body you see here is intended to stay true to Citroen's design values, with aerodynamics at their core. Minimal drag and lift is therefore vital, aided by gaping front intakes and that gigantic carbon diffuser at the rear. But its sheer presence is like nothing to have borne the firm's trademark chevrons before. As if a white Murciélago had been crossed with a vast albino lion, there's a weird, wild mix of Italian exotic and animal aggression.

Inside, it's a contrastingly dark, enveloping environment, minimal, ultra-high-tech and swathed with the sort of bold-but-bonkers conceit that only Citroen would dare: copper. There are bucket seats and a head-up display, the usual concessions to tomorrow's motoring modernity, but copper? It's partly highly polished and partly rough too, creating textures within textures, emotions on emotions. It shouldn't work anywhere, let alone in a bright white 25th-century supercar, but it does here.

Whether Citroen will take any of this experimentation on to its production lines remains to be seen, and the GTbC's place in a game hell-bent on realism is questionable, to say the least. The significance of the project is unequivocal, however. This new collusion between car and game designers offers car manufacturer – and, more critically, car buyer – the opportunity to experience what these once-otherworldly concepts can offer us in the here and now. "It's not a message that we're going to do something like this in the future," stresses Vidal. But the future is here, Gilles, and you've already done it. TG

'THE GTbC IS MEANT TO STAY TRUE TO CITROEN'S VALUES, BUT IT'S LIKE NOTHING TO HAVE BORNE THE FIRM'S CHEVRONS BEFORE'

IS IT JUST US, OR DOES THIS LOOK LIKE THE KIND OF MASKS KIDS WEAR AT HALLOWEEN?

The Battles

It's a great privilege to be able to step from one supercar and jump straight into another – a rival. You get an instant feel for the differences: how they accelerate, brake and steer; what they're like to simply sit in; how the instruments and controls work; how the materials feel.

Then, after a great deal of argument and counter-argument, you reach a conclusion. Of course, it's all subjective in the end – some buyers might be influenced by such tiny details as paint colours or a styling feature – but for Top Gear, there can only be one winner. Read on.

Need a reason why you should start following GT racing? How about 10 of the hottest cars from GT3 and one ruthlessly focussed Stig...

STIG

SIMPSON.

Words: Bill Thomas Photography: Lee Brimble, Joe Windsor-Williams

HEAVEN

THERE IS A LIME GREEN SHAPE IN MY mirrors getting closer in big edits and it must be The Stig in an Alpina B6. I had a feeling Stig would pick that car to drive first: along with the Audi R8 V10, it's the newest thing here, and therefore the most interesting for the Stiglet's brain.

I am driving a Ford GT – slowly by Stig standards, like a mewing pussy in someone else's expensive racing car, backing off early, not using the brakes, trying to get a feel without pushing beyond my own very limited limits – and am about to get out of the way of The Stig in a clean and gentlemanly fashion, because upsetting his concentration and blocking him when he's on a quick one would not be advisable. He has been known to get angry with people who get in his way. Very angry.

We're on the main straight at Paul Ricard circuit in France, on the approach to the chicane halfway along it. Stig's exit speed out of the kink leading onto this straight is phenomenal – he is gaining on me like I am stuck in neutral. I ease off, give him the line into the chicane and note his braking point. Heinously late. Then he hurls the big lime car at the apexes, left, right, left, the Alpina's rear end twitches on entry, twitches on exit, and he's away up the next straight, hard on the gas and carrying more speed than I can fully understand. By God, he's fast. And he's only just got started...

Welcome to GT3 cars, up close and personal, the greatest names in supercars all in the one place. We're pretty revved up about the FIA GT3 series here at *Top Gear*, and it won't take long to explain why... it helps that all but one of the teams have let us have a go in their cars. More on that a bit later.

First, some explanation of what this championship is all about. You know what a Porsche 911 GT3 is, right? A stripped-out, lighter, meaner, more powerful, more track-focussed 911. Well, that's

what all of the cars you see on these pages are like too. Near-standard spec road car engines, with minor stuff done to the exhausts and electronics, mated to sequential racing gearboxes, sitting in minorly tweaked chassis and bodywork, stripped out and sprinkled with the usual racing addenda, and bolted to the track with hard-looking aero in the form of some mighty rear wings and diffusers. They look good, sound good, and go hard.

These are cars we know about, cars we can relate to and adore, and the racing versions make the same noises as the ones we see on the road. The list of marques is impressive: Ferrari (430 Scuderia), Aston Martin (DBRS9), Porsche (911 GT3), Lamborghini (Gallardo), Ford (GT), Corvette (Z06), Dodge (Viper), Alpina (B6), Ascari (KZ1R), Audi (R8 V10), Morgan (Aeromax) and Jaguar (XKRS).

That's 12, in case you weren't counting. And at the time of writing, the total number of cars confirmed for the grid at Silverstone is 44 (six Ferraris, six Porsches, six Fords, four Astons, four Audis, four Alpinas, four Corvettes, two Vipers, two Morgans, two Jags, two Ascaris and two Lambos).

The two-day session we're attending at Ricard is known as a Balance of Performance test. It's carried out by the SRO (Stéphane Ratel Organisation, the series organiser) and the FIA (*Federation Internationale d l'Automobile*, motorsport's world govening body) ›‹

'The Corvette might not be the quickest in a straight line, nor the most agile, but everything seems to gel better than in the others'

The hero and the hanger-on take a walk

One of Stig's relatives, Barry

AUDI R8 V10 LMS GT3
Price £239,901
Engine V10, mid
Capacity 4961cc
Power 540bhp @ 7800
Torque 229lb ft @ 4500
Weight 1200kg
Teams Rosberg, Phoenix

LAMBORGHINI GALLARDO GT3
Price £184,800
Engine V10, mid
Capacity 4961cc
Power 535bhp @ 7800
Torque 376lb ft @ 4500
Weight 1238kg
Team Reiter

CORVETTE Z06R GT3
Price £244,714
Engine V8, front
Capacity 7011cc
Power 510bhp @ 6000
Torque 480lb ft @ 4900
Weight 1272kg
Teams Callaway, Sourd

FERRARI 430 SCUDERIA
Price £192,431
Engine V8, mid
Capacity 4308cc
Power 520bhp @ 8500
Torque 342lb ft @ 5250
Weight 1219kg
Teams Kessel, JMB, CRS

ASTON MARTI DBRS9 GT3
Price £230,932
Engine V12, fron
Capacity 5944c
Power 550bhp @ 62
Torque 472lb ft @ 55
Weight 1300kg
Teams Hexis, Brix

ASCARI KZ1R GT3
Price £166,320
Engine V8, mid
Capacity 4991cc
Power 502bhp @ 7500
Torque 405lb ft @ 4500
Weight 1200kg
Teams CRS, ARL

FORD GT GT3
Price £322,943
Engine V8, mid
Capacity 5409cc
Power 550bhp @ 7600
Torque 457lb ft @ 6000
Weight 1160kg
Teams Matech, Fischer

PORSCHE 911 997 GT3 CUP S
Price £240,097
Engine flat 6, rear
Capacity 3797cc
Power 440bhp @ 8000
Torque 229lb ft @ 7250
Weight 1150kg
Teams Prospeed, Muhlner

VIPER COMPETITION COUPE
Price £212,520
Engine V10, front
Capacity 8284cc
Power 520bhp @ 5600
Torque 538lb ft @ 4500
Weight 1315kg
Team Zakspeed

BMW ALPINA B6 GT3
Price £328,847
Engine V8, front
Capacity 4398cc
Power 530bhp @ 55
Torque 534lb ft @ 4
Weight 1350kg
Team Alpina

Rictus grin from racing has yet to wear off

'Drivers are ranked gold, silver or bronze, depending on their experience and current level of racing expertise. But all the guys are quick'

and it does just that – keeps the performance of the cars as equal and as balanced as possible. You might think this is impure and against the nature of the sport, but you'd be wrong. What it does is throw more emphasis on the drivers and teams to get the maximum out of their cars at each event, to set them up as best as possible and use whatever tactical advantages they can to eke out wins. And of course, it keeps the racing close.

Balancing the cars' performance is no easy task. It is the job of two FIA-appointed drivers, Jean-Marc Gounon and Christophe Bouchut. Both are vastly experienced and talented GT drivers who know the cars well. They are also aware of any tricks the teams might pull to make the cars a little slower. This is a test in which, unofficially, the teams don't want their cars to go *too* quickly. But, outwardly at least, they're genuine and straightforward with the cars, and present them to the FIA ready to go and set up properly. Another test takes place at Monteblanco in Spain, which is more of a twisting circuit than Paul Ricard. Jaguar and Morgan weren't present at this event, but will turn up in Spain with their XKRS and Aero 8. From there, the times and traces and even factors like tyre wear are analysed, and the numbers crunched by computer. Only then do the cars receive ballast penalties to equalise them.

There are other interesting ideas at work here to keep the racing close. All drivers in the series are ranked gold, silver or bronze, depending on their past experience and current level of racing expertise. A gold driver is a top-notch semi-pro who is not considered a fully-fledged works driver, but may have raced professionally in the past. A silver driver is one level down from that, perhaps a younger pilot wanting to break into higher echelons of the sport, or an exceptionally good amateur, and bronze are the gentleman drivers, wealthy amateurs who are there for the fun of it and may be funding the team.

A car can be run by a combination of either a gold and bronze driver, or two silver drivers, but never two golds. Of course, all of these guys are quick, even the bronze-ranking drivers, but none of the cars will ⁞

ever be driven by full-on demon professional heroes who will jump in and dominate: Audi won't be able to run Allan McNish, for instance.

There are two races per meeting (see event calendar on p32) lasting an hour each. Last year's driver's championship was won by James Ruffler and Arnaud Peyroles in the Martini Callaway Corvette Z06R, while the manufacturers' championship was claimed by Matech GT Racing in the Ford GT. We had a beady eye on the series as it progressed, and so it seems did others: now Alpina and the might of Audi are here for 2009, and it seems that GT3s are really come of age. If you can't relate to F1, and find touring cars are too slow, this is the series for you. None are full works operations, of course, because that's not the way it works. However, the customers who buy these newest cars will surely be at the pointy end of the grid. The Audi especially looks quick.

It was indeed The Stig in the Alpina that had flown by. After my run in the GT – the first car of the day – I wandered down to the Alpina pit and watched Stig come in, swinging the car round in an easy arc to be pushed backward into the garage by the mechanics. And then something strange happened. Stig unstrapped his belts, opened the door and stood up, and a bunch of Alpina engineers swarmed around him. They jotted down notes on their clipboards as he talked about the car, giving his impressions on its set-up. The mysterious man in white held court, and the engineers they did listen. None of the Alpina team knew the identity of Stig, of course, but they knew *what* he was and had seen him on the telly in Germany. And so they scrawled their precious notes. Stigster had driven that car as fast as it would go, of course, and with such a new and unproven car, every bit of feedback was gold dust for the team. Apparently he had real issues with the stability of the rear end, which was enough for me to give that car a miss and try another one.

It is a great testimony to the openness and down-to-earth nature of the GT3 championship that the teams allowed us – one brilliant driver and one Numpty – to get behind the wheel of their precious cars. They just lined them up at the appropriate time ⠿

'The Aston is quite an animal too, one that you really have to muscle around the track, but one that rewards you once you're happy with it'

and let us rip for a few laps. Only the stuck-up corporate behemoth that is Audi refused to let us have a go, annoyingly, for reasons that made no sense at all – something to do with it not being 'fully developed'. Rubbish. Maybe the first drive of the V10 GT3 had been promised to some German media or other, who knows? Maybe we'll drive it some other time. Or not. Stig sat in it for a while for the photos and his body language spelt 'frustration'.

Still, there were plenty of other amazing machines to get to grips with. First the dark blue GT, low and wide and evil, lurking in its pit garage. With belts set to 'plump', I was soon made comfortable by the team and drivers. You feel very much enclosed and claustrophobic in a supercar racer like this. Visibility isn't good in any direction except forward, and the sloping A-pillars make it difficult to see the corner apexes. You sit low, too, and the racing seat encroaches on the sides of your helmet. The gearshift lever is big and tall and located immediately to the right of the small suede-covered wheel, through which you see a Stack digital display giving you various temperature readouts, revs, times and speeds. It's all functional and spare. The belt buckles clank and echo in the stripped-out metallic cockpit.

The Ford GT GT3 is a fabulous car – no wonder it won the team championship last year. It is stable and solid and has plenty of grip at all speeds. Stig reckoned it's developing a good deal of downforce. The thing does feel jammed to the track. Engine power feels enormous initially, but I learned later that, by the standards of the other cars here, it probably isn't the fastest in a straight line. What it does have is sublime throttle feel, and it delivers its power and torque in a beautifully linear and predictable way. I loved this car instantly and didn't want to get out of it. It is *so* stable. The gearshift is extraordinary. You use the clutch for pulling away and for downshifts only. For upshifts, just leave your

foot on the throttle and jam the lever toward you. It cuts the engine for a microsecond before engaging the next gear, with magical smoothness.

The Ferrari felt most like a road car, most familiar. I drove last year's F430 GT3 while Stig had a run in the new Scuderia. He was lining up to set the fastest time of the day when his Scud started to cough and nearly ran out of fuel. This annoyed Stig intensely and he wondered whether the team had short-fuelled him deliberately to stop him going fastest. The Ferrari, in 430 Scud form, is definitely the most rapid thing here, and also the easiest to drive. You sit up relatively high in a spacious cabin and the paddle shifts on the wheel – no clutch, remember – make things pretty simple. It feels pointy at the front end, delicate and light, much more so than the solid-feeling Ford. It's more like a single-seater at turn-in, nose-led, and the brakes are the most powerful of the cars here. Stig, and every person in the pit lane, was convinced that this new Scuderia is the fastest thing here, maybe just a little bit quicker than the Audi. The team didn't have a dedicated driver present on the day, unlike Audi, so the Scud didn't set a scintillating time, but it was fastest in the hands of Gounon.

It's amazing how different in character these cars are. The Porsche was the only car I stalled. The Aston was the only car I span. These two were the most difficult to go quickly in, the most unforgiving. I called the Porsche 'spiky' in my notes. It's not there to help you. It's a hard, steely, mechanical device that needs mastering. It makes probably the best noise from the inside of any of the cars, its shrill high-revving flat-six a true masterwork.

'The Ford GT GT3 is a fabulous car – no wonder it won the championship last year. It is stable and solid and has plenty of grip'

I'll take the Aston, you can have the Alpina

And the Aston is quite an animal too, one that you really have to muscle around the track but one that probably rewards you with great balance and pace once you'd got comfortable in it. I never did, really, and a slight delay on the gearshift indicator meant that I went down one too many gears into the chicane and rotated. Numpty.

As Stig drove the Viper – I missed out, another small technical delay – I listened to him and the rest of the cars roar past and noted their sounds, then closed my eyes and tried to pick them. They all have distinctive and utterly awesome exhaust notes. The four that are most similar are the Corvette, Ascari, GT and Alpina, with their hard NASCAR-style V8 roars. The Alpina has a supercharger whistle, though, so that's easier to pick. The Viper, Gallardo and Audi V10s have a lovely, almost mellow mid-pitch howl, the Porsche a shrill bark that penetrates to the centre of your head, and the Ferrari an even higher-pitched yell again, while the big Aston V12 sits somewhere between the Ferrari and the V8s in tone and is perhaps the most stirring of them all. When 44 of them – *forty-four!* – are screaming by in a big pack, the sound will be one of the best in racing, anywhere.

Stig reckoned the Viper had the potential to go fastest if the full fury of its 8.3-litre V10 was unleashed – it's heavily detuned in a GT3. But I was finding it difficult to concentrate on what he

was saying because I was enraptured with the car I'd just tried, the Ascari, which felt totally natural to drive. It is the only one of these cars with a carbon-fibre chassis, and it shows. It is fabulously stiff torsionally, light too, yet the suspension set-up the guys were using was soft. The car was utterly fluid, riding the kerbs as if they weren't there, and it became my favourite car to that point. Inside, the big old-shape BMW M5 5.0-litre V8 had a staccato thrum to it, almost like an easy-revving twin-cylinder motorbike. This car might steal the title this year. Watch it.

But the car I was looking forward to the most came at the very end of the day. Stig went out in it first, and I stood on the pitwall with an engineer and timed him. A 2.09 dead on his first flyer. Then a 2.08.5. Then a 2.08 dead, which was the fastest time up until that point. And then he came in early and gave three extra flying laps to me. Generous soul.

It was the Corvette, of course, the driver's championship-winning car. Having seen countless Corvettes winning at Le Mans over the years, it had even more resonance than the Aston or Porsche. It might not be the quickest in a straight line, nor the most agile, but everything seems to gel better than in the other cars. It was the racer I could best imagine doing a very long stint in, the polar opposite of the Porsche because I felt it was on my side. Good visibility, good brakes and

balance, easy throttle response and an enormous slug of torque down low combined with some seriously fast and urgent revving. And the soundtrack? Well, try a YouTube search for 'LG Motorsports Gigliotti Corvette C6 W Challenge 2007 Utah' and you'll get the idea.

I did eight laps and staggered away from it bathed in sweat. I had not gone fast – probably eight seconds slower than The Stig's incredible laps – but I had been confident, and the car was faithful from the off. If I was to choose any of these cars to race, it would be Corvette first, Ascari second and Ferrari third. Stig wouldn't race anything but the Ferrari, because it's the fastest. But that's Stig.

The Audi went out later in the day and beat Stig's Corvette lap time, but by that stage he'd left the circuit, wandering off in the direction of Plan d'Aups Sainte Baume, his appetite sated. Thank you GT3s. Thanks for the greatest day we've ever had.

Photography by John Wycherley

Somehow, Bill Thomas manages to get hold of three of the world's most famous cars to thrash them in the Italian mountains

Supercars
On Ice

WHERE DO YOU START WITH CARS like these? Well, in this case, we started with an early flight from Gatwick to Bologna. We were met at Bologna airport by Alfredo from Land Rover Italy, who gave us a Freelander diesel to drive for a few days. We set the Freelander's satnav to take us to a destination in Sant'Agata, then on to another destination in Maranello. Simple. A flight, a couple of waypoints, normal procedure. Routine stuff. We were so excited, we nearly shat ourselves.

Once outside the airport and trundling along in the trusty Landy – a vehicle we'd grow to adore over the next three days – we phoned Mauro Calo, the safe pair of hands who'd been given the rotten task of driving a black £160,000 Aston Martin DBS down to northern Italy from *Top Gear* HQ in London. He was near Sant'Agata already. We agreed he

should park discreetly nearby and wander up to the Lamborghini factory on foot – best not drop a DBS right into the visitor's parking area of a rival supercar maker. They don't like comparison tests much, the Italians.

When Mauro turned up, Schofield: driver, Norris: art director, Wycherley: photographer and yours truly: writer, were wandering round in a kind of trance in the Lamborghini factory museum, gazing at Uraccos and Miuras and Countaches and Diablos. We five car-loving numbnuts were in hog heaven, feeling just how *you* would feel: expectant and thrilled and wondering what on earth we'd done to deserve all this. For at that moment, there was a 99.9 per cent chance that Lamborghini would give us a £192,000 Murciélago LP640 to punt around an ice track and thrash through the hills of northern Italy for a few days.

Half an hour after that, there was a 99.9 percent chance that Ferrari would give us a £179,000 599 Fiorano to punt around an ice track and thrash through the hills of northern Italy for a few days. We'd have appreciated the diesel Freelander on its own, but these three? This was fever. Somehow, I'll have to swallow my guilt at being there without you, and tell you what these mighty supercars are like to punt around an ice track and thrash through the hills of northern Italy for a few days.

Soon, all three supercars were sitting side by side in a little square in Maranello centre – that'll be 18,430cc, 1752bhp, £531,502 and 604mph in one tiny car park, with five happy car-loving numbnuts scurrying around like over-excited dogs, not quite knowing where to look or where to pee. The three greatest supercars on earth? No arguments here. ∴

Synchronising radios to make constant swearing and jokes an annoying reality

You really want to give us one of those? Are you sure? Yeah? OK, we'll take it, thanks a lot, bye

Take it and thrash it - Ferrari 599 thrives on high revs and hard living

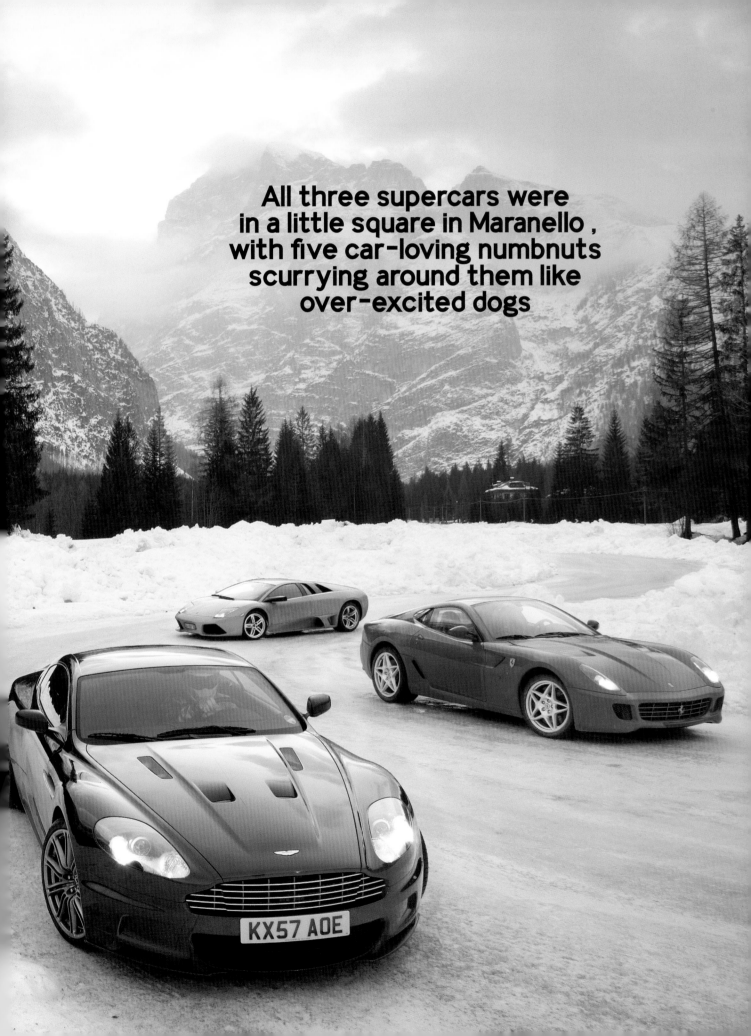

All three supercars were in a little square in Maranello , with five car-loving numbnuts scurrying around them like over-excited dogs

There isn't really a fourth car for this comparo, because nothing quite makes the cut. We thought about a Continental GT Speed, but Bentley wasn't flexible enough to get us one in time, and we thought it too heavy, anyway, despite its 600bhp and 12 cylinders. We were tempted by Paganis and Ascaris and Koenigseggs, but they don't have the right names or the right heritage, and they're all a bit sharp and pointy. And no, not even Porsche can play at this party. The 523bhp, £131,000, 204mph GT2 raises a plaintive hand, but a pumped-up 911 is ultimately not special or exclusive enough in this exalted company. And it fails spectacularly at being a V12. Sorry. Aston Martin, Lamborghini and Ferrari are up there in the rarified supercar stratosphere, beyond Porsche's ceiling, whether the proud Germans like it or not. For now, these three great marques fight it out alone. They deserve to.

OK, let's weigh them up, crunch the numbers and get them straight. Have a look at the spec panel on page 101 to get the basics. Weights pretty even; engine capacity pretty even; power in a sliding scale, with the Aston trailing by over 100bhp; prices in orbit.

What you can't see on that panel is that the Lambo makes its extraordinary 631bhp maximum at 8,000rpm, and its max torque at 6,000rpm. It's difficult to imagine a 6.5-litre V12 revving to such a frenzied height, but it does, rampantly, loving every extra thou.

The 599's engine is similar, based on that of the Enzo. Good starting point. It makes its 620bhp max at 7,600rpm and peak torque comes at 5,600rpm. Another revver, then, but it feels punchier low down in the rev range than the Lambo, and it's almost an exaggerated, semi-artificial super-punch of torque, the kind that Kimi probably likes in his F1 car. You can feel cutting-edge engine mapping at work here.

The DBS's motor is sensational, too. It probably sounds even more entrancing than the Italians, more mellow and tuneful. Even though it makes its 510bhp

Imagine being in a DBS and happening across these two crazy bastards

at 6,500rpm and max torque punches in at a high 5,750rpm, the thrust seems to happen from zero rpm, as soon as you breathe on the throttle. For that reason, you never feel you're getting left behind if you're chasing down the Italians on give and take roads. Wonder what all of this revviness and high-end power will be like on sheet ice? Time to find out...

Our first destination was Auronzo, where there is a brilliant little ice karting track and, more importantly for us, a full-sized one for cars as well. I don't know how The Stig finds out about these things, but as we stopped to take some static shots of the cars before we binned them, he came walking briskly out of a forest, climbed straight into the Aston – the only car on summer tyres, and therefore by far the trickiest – and proceeded to reel off four perfect laps. Sideways everywhere, natch, even on the straight bits. He did the same in the Ferrari, then the Lambo, then walked off in the direction of Cimon del Froppa.

Time to admit that our cover image is a fantasy, a complete set-up. Sorry. The Stig didn't crash these cars, but you probably guessed that. More surprising is that we didn't, either. We tried our very best to destroy them, but narrowly avoided it. Driving a car worth £192,000 around corners with a co-efficient of grip too low to walk on doesn't teach you much, other than the meaning of fear. How The Stig did those laps without any sort of build-up or gauge for the grip level will remain a mystery until I croak.

As The Stig's race suit blended with the snow and the trees and he went off to climb sheer 5,000ft-high rock-faces or whatever it is he does in the winter, it was time to attack some tarmac. The roads in the Dolomites around Cortina are a mixture – tight point-and-squirt switchbacks climbing up the side of valleys between ski resorts; more open, faster sweeping roads running along the valley walls; and further south toward Bologna, super-fast dual carriageways spearing between mountain cliffs. Not all of these roads are appropriate or easy for near-200mph supercars, but they're all tremendous fun.

So. If someone approached you on a fine winter's morning holding the keys to these three cars, which would you choose? The answer is that you wouldn't care. And not only because you'd know you'd be swapping those keys at various points during the day. ∵

You can't fake this face - Norris concentrating hard

Ferrari cylinders above, Aston cylinders below

You, Mr Lambo, are coming over all mid-engined and superior now

You want more cylinders? OK, then how about these puppies?

Lambo is colour-coordinated with snow-depth poles: of course, dahlink

Sidewaysness in a 611bhp car with every driver aid turned right off

Stig fixes a gimlet eye on the distant supercars and squeaks slightly

Even at the end of the test, after many hundreds of clicks, we five car-loving numbnuts couldn't have cared less which car we chose. They do different jobs, they have different natures – all are great.

It can be boiled down to this: the Aston is a work of art, the Lambo a sledgehammer, and the 599 a scalpel. Picking a winner is impossible. If you had £160,000 to blow on a car, it's likely you might have £531,902 to blow on all three. And that's the answer.

If ever an employee would be biased, you'd think it might be an employee of Ferrari – probably the best-known Italian company and perhaps the one held in the highest esteem. Working for the Prancing Horse must be like working at the Vatican. And even the Ferrari tech guy who helped fit 'our' 599's winter tyres for the ice track work had to admit that the DBS was beautiful. He may have even said that it was better to look at than his beloved Fiorano, though I could never quote him on that.

"It is verry bew-tee-full, ziss Ass-tonne-Marr-teen," said the Italian, properly awed.

Slot in behind the big steering wheel, and you're immediately comfortable, surrounded by beautiful ornamentation and sculpture and some of the highest-grade leather anywhere. Punch the fat key fob into its slot in the middle of the dash, push and hold, and the V12 blips into life. Everything feels very natural. Next, into the Lambo. This is like nothing else. Upward-lifting scissor doors are an event every time you use them, an intro to the weird world of the LP640. You slide down low into the bucket, pull the door down with a thunk. The wheel seems about 17 miles from the instrument panel, with the base of the windscreen another 85 miles beyond that. The roofline is low, but doesn't encroach too much, even if you're over six feet tall. Turn the key, and she roars into life after a long, deep whirr from the starter motor. I bet that starter motor develops more power than your average Astra VXR.

The Ferrari is the most saloon-like of these cars to sit in. It is tall and wide, and the visibility is good. You start the engine with a button on the steering wheel, which also has its manettino lozenge for onboard transmission, differential and stability control system settings – plus a row of bright red lights in its carbon-fibre top to tell you you're approaching 9,000rpm – 9,000rpm in a 6.0-litre V12, let's not forget. It all says cutting-edge tech, a direction Ferrari seems to be making its own, and if they say it's a direct hand-down from F1, we can believe them. The paddle shift blades, like those of the Lambo, are attached to the steering column, not the wheel. I don't understand why – it would be much better to be able to keep your hands on the wheel and change gear with paddles attached to it.

These cars are evenly matched on most roads – it's only at extremely high speeds that the Aston begins to ⠿

Look closely and note filth: never have cars like these been so dirty

Aston, Lambo and Ferrari are up there in the rarified supercar stratosphere, beyond Porsche's ceiling, whether the Germans like it or not

Lambo	£192,000	6496cc	631bhp	487lb ft	1665kg	3.3 to 60	7.8 to 100	211mph
Ferrari	£179,902	5999cc	611bhp	448lb ft	1688kg	3.5 to 60	7.4 to 100	205mph
Aston	£160,000	5935cc	510bhp	420lb ft	1695kg	4.2 to 60	9.4 to 100	188mph

The Stig not keen on static imagery. Only ice and speed

More filth (on the cars) and they love it, oh yes they do

The Stig, waiting. On summer tyres, the DBS was the most 'interesting'

get left behind, which you'd expect given its power deficit. For the rest of the time, its ample torque keeps it in the hunt, though it's not as good at getting its power down as either the four-wheel-drive Lambo or the tricked-up, high-tech 599 with its e-diff. There is something ever so slightly bizarre going on at the back of the DBS, as if the active dampers are set to do something weird to keep the tyres stuck to the road. Everything else seems well tied down, including the steering, which lacks the Ferrari's quickness but matches the Lambo for feel. Schofield fell in love with the Aston and stayed in love. "And you don't feel a prat in this car," he muttered at one stage, an indirect swipe at the other two cars, maybe, and some of their owners.

Still, it would have taken a fire crew and a cutting tool to remove Calo from the Lambo. For him, the brutal, shocking, wonderful, weird way was the only way. The Lambo summed up what Italian supercars should be all about – drama, power and exploding pedestrian heads with visual shock. And he's not wrong.

But because I'm holding the pencil, I'll have the final word, and for me, the Ferrari was the car I'd keep forever. You can go deeper into corners with this car, push harder and harder and never quite feel the thing will bite you, even with 611bhp on tap – for instance, you can flick it. *Flick* a 1,688kg supercar. You can't flick the others like this. The steering is lightning-quick, feeling almost too light at first, but push on and you begin to understand what it's about – agility, combined with a lack of nervousness at high cruising speed. All the while, the gearshift is eye-blink quick when you need it to be, or thought-free automatic at other times, and the auto clutch works perfectly at parking speeds. For me, this 599 is a work of high magic – it will take a place in history among the greatest Ferraris, because it somehow combines the docile nature of a grand tourer with the soul of an F1 car. And it has a boot.

But is it really the best car? Of course it isn't. The other two are far too mighty for that. It probably says it all that The Stig did precisely four laps in each...

If someone approached you on a fine winter's morning holding the keys to these cars, which would you choose? The answer is that you wouldn't care

Note snow-depth poles. Just avoid hitting them, and all will be super

LIGHT

Three very light, very fast weapons head to the *Top Gear* track. Jason Barlow dons a helmet and joins The Stig

SABRES

Photography by Lee Brimble

THESE CARS ARE THE FUTURE. No, seriously. Almost 51 years since the Lotus Seven first appeared, and 35 since Caterham started 'finessing' its basic formula, this sort of thing now makes more sense than ever. Yes, even the borderline-psychotic R500.

Think about it. Something unpleasant is in the geopolitical/military-industrial ether, and driving just isn't as much fun as it should be. If it isn't congestion, it's the fact that petrol stations now employ mortgage advisers to help you pay for a tank of unleaded. And if it isn't that, it's the creeping realisation that combusting a refined, oil-based product in order to travel 30,000 miles a year with some carpet samples in the boot is, you know, so last century.

Is there an up-side to any of this? Well, yes. Use public transport in the city (go on, it's not bad), and work from home more often (that's what broadband's for). This will a) help your work/life balance and b) put driving just for the hell of it back on the agenda, which is where the Caterham R500, Ariel Atom 3 and hot new KTM X-Bow come into the equation. OK, so a used Golf or Focus is going to be useful back-up but, really, what else do you need?

"Power makes you faster on the straights. Subtracting weight makes you faster everywhere," Colin Chapman once said. I wonder what he'd

make of this latest version of his first really bright idea, which is now both lighter *and* more powerful. If it's the fun of driving you want to re-engage with, then 263bhp in something that weighs 506kg ought to do the trick. Crunch the numbers, and you get 520bhp per tonne, which is Bugatti Veyron territory (power-to-weight being the main barometer of driving fun, not horsepower). Not bad, when motive force comes courtesy of a juicily reworked version of Ford's proletarian 2.0-litre, four-pot Duratec powertrain.

You have to marvel at Caterham's ability to tickle Chapman's minimalism into increasingly mind-bending forms. But if you're buying into the whole lightweight deal as the Future (with a capital F) – and I hope you are – then the paragon isn't a modified version of a 51-year-old blueprint, it's the brand new KTM X-Bow. It has a carbon-fibre monocoque, and the bloke who developed the Veyron worked on the chassis tuning. The car appeared three times in the pages of *Top Gear* in as many issues, and with good reason. We like it. A lot.

Now it lines up against the R500 and the other car that has taken Chapman's famous "Simplicate, then add lightness" mantra and turned it into a new religion: the Ariel Atom. Ariel shares its name with a leading washing powder, but it's a bit more interesting. The Atom 3 features lots of detail changes (among other things, its latticed, er, body

has a different shape to create a roomier cockpit) and a supercharged version of the latest Honda Civic Type-R engine, which includes twin balancer shafts for improved refinement.

Mind you, with close to 320bhp and a shockingly skinny 460kg kerb weight, refinement is unlikely to be top of your list of requirements. The Atom's PtW stats are off the scale: 696bhp per tonne. This thing is so absurdly light that an extra pie at lunchtime really could blunt the 0–60 time by a few tenths.

There will be no pies this lunchtime, however. Because we've come to the *Top Gear* track to get to grips with these three, together for the first ⁚⁚

The Stig does *Exorcist*-style head turn to keep eye on opponents

Exhaust on KTM is compact and out of the way, unlike Caterham's

'The Atom's PtW stats are off the scale: 696bhp per tonne. This thing is so absurdly light that an extra pie at lunchtime could blunt the 0-60 time'

GO20PA

Stigster creates a smoke-screen to further confuse those on his tail

CATERHAM R500
Price £36,995
Capacity 1999cc
Bhp 263bhp
Torque 177lb ft
Weight 506kg
0–62mph 2.8secs
Top speed 150mph

KTM X-BOW
Price £53,880
Capacity 1984cc
Bhp 240bhp
Torque 229lb ft
Weight 790kg
0–62mph 3.9secs

ARIEL ATOM SUPERCHARGED
Price £34,949
Capacity 1998cc
Bhp 318bhp
Torque 177lb ft
Weight 460kg
0–62mph 2.8secs
Top speed 155mph

Cars so light, they make a rowing cox look like a Bulgarian female shotputter

time, with The Stig here as mentor. And as everyone knows, The Stig doesn't do lunch.

Good job too: these cars all clearly favour the more snake-hipped driver. As the most obviously 'designed' of the trio, the X-Bow is the easiest one to get in and out of. Being able to stand on the carbon-fibre sills before climbing in is a good party trick too; after which, it's feet on the bespoke (fixed) Recaro (moulded) seat, then slide in. Easy. The pedal box is attached to an adjustable panel, and the steering wheel detaches, so there's race-car style drama without the need for human origami. The X-Bow pulses with hi-tech, and, like all purpose-made tools, there's a carefully tailored feel to it. It immediately feels like a bodily extension. And whatever you do, the wheel still ends up in your chest, just like in a proper racing car.

The R500 is less impressive. You've got to watch yourself on the Caterham's side-exit exhausts (hot), and even with my best poseur's Alpinestars race boots on, my size 11 feet are still too big for the pedals. The four-point harness is a nuisance too, and there's lots of heat soak through the bulkhead and transmission tunnel. Elbow room is tight. Yep, like every Caterham I've ever driven – including the wide-body CSR – the R500 visits new and unusual ergonomic punishments on the driver. Then again, masochism has always been part of the attraction...

Given that the Ariel is a barely-there web of welded steel tubing, getting in and out is no problem. Excess heat in the interior isn't an issue either, because there aren't any body panels – or much of an interior, come to think of it. But the seats are hard, and the driving position isn't as snug as the Caterham's or as purposeful as the X-Bow's. Crucially, though, the Atom 3, with its wider cockpit, is the lightweight car that best suits heavyweight humans. Fat blokes will fit in here. They'll struggle in the others.

What all these cars deliver, though, is a driving experience that is unparalleled. They might all cost the wrong side of 35 grand, but their ability to put a big, dumb grin on your face makes them priceless in today's grumpy world.

All three generate purest street theatre. No point getting too deep into the aesthetics: how they look is :

'What all these cars deliver, is a driving experience that is unparalleled. Their ability to put a grin on your face makes them priceless in this grumpy world'

When separated from the car, Stig suffers his own reduction in power

peripheral to how they go. Oddly, I was drawn most to the R500, with its stripes and carbon nose cone and front cycle wings. This thing might even qualify for 'icon' status by now. And there's nothing to beat the feeling you get when your backside is perched barely an inch off the back axle.

The X-Bow and Ariel are properly modern, especially the KTM. But it's also a bit visually random; exceptionally well-made, but with its innards and gizzards exposed in a way that's standard operating procedure on a bike but a bit odd on a car. Orange is KTM's trademark colour, but in black the X-Bow looks less like an exotic fly and more like a Lockheed SR-71.

For cars that are, on the face of it, so similar in philosophy, they don't half feel different when you start to push them. The X-Bow confused the hell out of me first time out back at the Ascari circuit in May, but on the *TG* track it all clicks perfectly. Yes, it's a bit soft, but its chassis is truly sublime. Weighing in at 790kg, and with less power (240bhp) than the R500 or Atom 3, it's obviously less frantic. But if 62mph in 3.9 seconds and 100 in around nine doesn't do it for you, then seek immediate psychiatric help.

Anyway, as I say, the chassis's the thing here. Into and through 'Hammerhead', the X-Bow is perfectly balanced; crisp turn-in, mild understeer to warn off the less confident pilot, then into beautifully telegraphed oversteer if you keep the power on. After which, you can just drift it all day long. It's brilliant. Initially, the KTM feels a little squishy, and there's an imprecision to its major controls – the fly-by-wire throttle is occasionally irritating – but it's alert and razor-sharp when you need it to be. This is a very, very nicely set-up car indeed, even in the standard trim in which we find it here (though it's worth pointing out that this car is fitted with the optional limited-slip diff). Running race settings, on sticky slick rubber, I'd say it would be a devastating weapon. What a pity it doesn't sound more exciting...

Which is where the R500 steps up. Its performance is explosive, and it sounds explosive. In fact, going anywhere in this thing is like being strapped to a series of explosions. It's intoxicating.

Driving the R500 like you mean it takes commitment and a little bravery, but it's not the treacherous, conniving little demon that I was half-expecting. This particular car is running the optional sequential six-speed gearbox, and it's sensational – pull back to change up; push forward to change down. You can forget the clutch for full-bore upshifts, which is fun, though downshifts are trickier; you need to heel and toe to match revs with gearbox speed, or risk locking up the rear end. Acceleration is demented; 0–62 takes 2.8 seconds, and it'll shed all that speed just as quickly. No mass, you see.

This, more than any other Caterham, takes serious mental recalibration. Everything happens so quickly that it's easy to react equally quickly, when actually what you have to do is slow all your inputs down. This is an easy car to overcook, but if you keep things measured and progressive, it's a life-affirming experience. Its Avon tyres (on 13in wheels!) generate lots of grip, but obviously it'll slide if you keep your foot in, and once you've got the hang of it, it's easier to play about with than you might think, despite the super-fast steering and tight slip angle. The R500 needs practice; the more you experiment, the better it gets. The perfect track car, then, but emphatically not the thing for a cheeky wet roundabout giggle: it'll bite.

And the Ariel? Well, the Atom 3 is just too extreme for me. The throttle-mapping feels odd, and, like the Caterham, you need to concentrate hard and modulate your inputs. Full throttle in first gear is not advisable. Second, third and fourth are only marginally less extreme, and the whole thing is a fairly knife-edge, on/off sort of experience. There's a new linkage on the 'box, and changes are even more rifle-bolt fast than before. Indeed, in terms of sheer naked exhilaration, the

Atom has the measure of the KTM and R500. Which, if you think about it, is no mean feat.

New engine mounts and that smoother Civic Type-R engine mean that the Atom is less of a blender at high speed, but it's still unlikely to be confused with, say, a Rolls-Royce Phantom. And though its handling is more progressive than on earlier incarnations, it's still hair-trigger stuff. On the 'Follow-through', I had one particularly hairy high-speed 'moment', and there's less margin for error. There's no doubt that Ariel has created a colossally exciting car, and, for the truly fearless, it might well be The One. But it can feel nervous, which makes me nervous.

Even so, what a thing it is. The Ariel man talks cheerfully about the X-Bow's arrival expanding the market, rather than pilfering his customers. Caterham, meanwhile, keeps on keeping on, and the R500 is proof of their specific genius. But the KTM is the new king here, a beautifully well developed machine that reaches out to the lightweight future and makes it that bit more realistic. Tick too many of the options boxes, and it could get expensive (our test car is £50,000+), and the X-Bow's chassis could definitely handle more power. It's not hardcore. But it's hard enough. *TG*

The X-Bow is the most user-friendly of the cars here. Least? The Atom

'The X-Bow is a very nicely set-up car. Running race settings, on slick rubber, it would be a devastating weapon. What a pity it doesn't sound more exciting'

Chapman's design is still as striking as ever. The R500 is the looker here

BAD
BOYS

632bhp vs 647bhp. 0-62mph in 3.4 seconds vs 0-62mph in 3.5 seconds. Lambo vs ZR1. Prepare yourselves for the most brutal supercar battle ever

Words: Paul Horrell photography: Lee Brimble

Above: Lambo sticks two doors up at the ZR1

Far right: keep an eye on the engine

Main: performance without the pretension is the ZR1's creed

Not the same hand-made interior as the Lambo

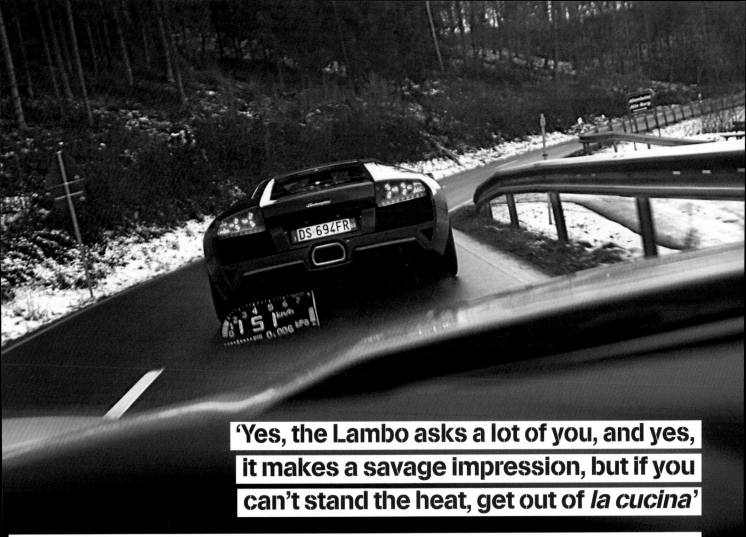

'Yes, the Lambo asks a lot of you, and yes, it makes a savage impression, but if you can't stand the heat, get out of *la cucina*'

FOR THE ITALIANS IN THIS DUEL, it's like a night at the opera. All the showiness and drama of La Scala. Huge cast, elaborate costumes, deep lungs, music by Puccini or Verdi. For the Americans, it's the straight-forwardness of a four-piece guitar band. Maybe the Killers. (Or are the Killers a bad choice of analogy? – 'Are We Human or Are We Dancer?' Not so very straightforward really. 'I've got Soul But I'm Not a Soldier' Huh? It was re-imagined by Bill Bailey as 'I've got Ham But I'm Not a Hamster'. Anyway, I digress.)

The Murciélago LP640 and Corvette ZR1 couldn't be more different. To their fans, both hold an extraordinary power to captivate and move. Both camps find the other a bit pointless.

Pointless? How in the blue blazes can any 200mph car be pointless? For the Corvette crowd, it's the attention-seeking cantankerousness of the Lambo that undermines it. Their beloved American idol is so easy to live with, you can use it all the time. That way, you can enjoy its pulverising acceleration and face-bending cornering whenever the opportunity presents itself. From the Corvette side of the fence, the Murciélago is such a demanding luvvy that you might just be tempted to leave the thing at home.

But to fans of the Lamborghini, that's the entire point of a Murciélago. Yes it asks an awful lot of you, and yes it makes a savage impression wherever it goes. It is a rolling event, a special occasion car, and you should feel privileged to be a part of the whole hysterical performance. If you can't stand the heat, get out of *la cucina*.

Of course, the Murciélago LP640 and the Corvette ZR1 do have something in common, and that's the reason we've brought them together: their huge power and hallucinatory speed. Let's get those astonishing figures out of the way, just to establish their *bone fides*. Lambo: 632bhp, 0-62 in 3.4secs, 210mph. ZR1: 647bhp, 0-62 in 3.5secs, 205mph. Not so very far apart eh?

But look at the differences. The Lambo has a mid-mounted normally aspirated V12, four-wheel drive and a flappy paddle transmission. The Corvette has a front-engined supercharged V8 driving the rear wheels. It might be slower away from rest while its 335-section tyres spin like Catherine wheels, but real-world acceleration is a different matter because it's some 150kg lighter than the Lambo.

Mind you, none of those technical differences goes even one per cent of the way to illustrating the real difference between these two cars. They just don't begin to explain the straightforwardness and sheer pragmatic approachability of the Corvette, or the outrageously demanding and domineering nature of the Lamborghini.

Just to climb into the Lambo is a palaver. The door swings up, you drop down into the strange skeletal seat, you pull down the door and the seat belt comes down from your inboard shoulder. The steering wheel is somewhere between your knees, your head bumps against the top of the door, you can't see to reverse unless you've specified the optional £2,585 chuff-cam. Basically, Lambo made space for the engine and transmission and wheels, styled a bizarrely dramatic shape to drape over them, and then chiselled out a small and inconvenient space for the person who's paying for it all and his or her probably slightly terrified companion.

The Corvette is, well, a car. Open the door, sit inside. Everything's where you'd expect it to be, including your luggage which simply goes in through the hatchback. You can see out. You can understand it all. The ride's not too punishing, and at normal speeds it isn't too noisy. The gearbox is slow, but none of the controls are heavy. The ZR1 is a ridiculously easy car to use in the ho-hum of everyday driving. The Lambo is anything but. It sets you on edge, what with its slightly bolshie e-gear transmission and colossal width and minimal ground clearance and ear-bleeding noise. ∴

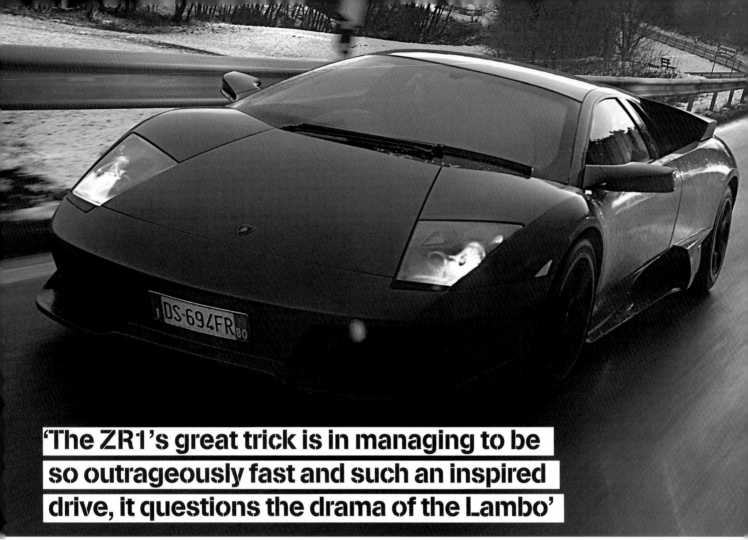

'The ZR1's great trick is in managing to be so outrageously fast and such an inspired drive, it questions the drama of the Lambo'

If you have the exuberance to match its limitless craziness, the Murciélago is a source of wonder that never dims. If you simply want to nip around the corner and park without drawing a crowd, it's an embarrassment. As you manoeuvre into place, all fizzing V12 tailpipe racket and smell of burning clutch, then open the scissor door and stumble inelegantly out, a hundred pairs of eyes are questioning your reproductive endowment and wondering if you're in the grip of a compensatory imperative.

The ZR1's great trick is in managing to be so outrageously fast and such an inspired drive that it calls into question the drama of the Murciélago. If a car can go as hard as this easy-going ZR1, why on earth does the Lambo need to be so

intimidating? The Corvette poses a nagging question about the Murciélago: at the centre of this Italian bluster, is there a hollow, false heart?

No. Categorically, there is not. The Lambo absolutely has the trousers to match its mouth. The engine, for a start, isn't just about shattering performance or an utterly captivating Richter-8 soundquake. It's also instantly responsive. But you do have to be paying attention: the power builds with every extra rev, especially beyond 5,000, and so the max power arrives at 8,000, the exact instant the rev limiter cuts in. So to get the best out of it you have to be right on the case with your gearchange timing.

Whatever, you're sure to be travelling at some hectic sort of pace when you start to explore the

cornering. And here the Murciélago sends you a surprise parcel. It isn't half as scary as you'd think. Provided you can see where the road goes (the A-posts get in the way) and you have enough tarmac (the rear end is disproportionately wider than the front), you'll be OK.

Its steering is just sublime: you can pour the Murciélago into corners and commune intimately with the front tyre treads, sensing exactly how much grip they can call on. It begins with gentle understeer, but you've always got the power to settle things. Don't delude yourself though: this is not a car you ever slide. Step beyond its comfort zone and it will turn as scary as it looks. Live within it, and there's the balance and feel of a sort of Impreza squared. ∴

Lambo continues
abuse of ZR1
behind its back

Above: that ZR1
engine offers
up 647bhp

Bottom right:
four-wheel drive
means über grip

Main: the brave
American sticks to
the showy Italian

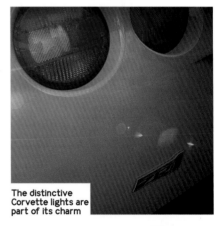

The distinctive
Corvette lights are
part of its charm

The sheer force of the Murciélago's acceleration and braking and cornering grip, and the subtler sensory array of noise and steering feel, make for an experience that takes everything we love about cars and goes beyond it. Truly, a supercar.

Can the Corvette answer all this? Oh yes. But it's more traditional. And, when you're really pushing on, it's actually got the trickier chassis to keep on top of. That's because its steering is fast and a little nervous – the car's set up to be so agile that on the road I find myself wishing for a little gentle front-end slip in the first few degrees of a corner, just to let me know how adhesive things are down at the front tyres. And of course it's rear-drive, which means you can't just stuff down the throttle and expect the car to sort it all out. Apple-pie drifts are there for the taking when the ESP is off, or even when it's in the intermediate 'competitive mode'.

Set it up right though and the mid-bend balance and damping control are sublime. If you really want to get out of a corner sharpish, wait until the apex is well behind you and squeeze the loud pedal progressively. The Vette rewards it with magnetic traction – aided by clever adaptive damping and the balanced weight distribution from its rear-mounted gearbox. You're projected away in a drastic, drastic dollop of get-up-and-go.

Thank its supercharger for the ZR1's rocket thrust. While the Lambo has 6.5 litres, the Corvette has almost as much at 6.2, but the lungs of the blower mean you never really need to rev the Corvette to get a brutal episode of acceleration. Just as well actually, for the six-speed gearbox is on the clunky side. Just stick it in the highest gear you think you're going to need for the foreseeable, and look down on the world from that high-altitude torque curve. Truth is, in a world where automated-clutch and twin-clutch transmissions are becoming the supercar norm, the ZR1's manual box is about the one remaining thing to call low-tech. The chassis and suspension is aluminium, the body carbon, parts of the engine titanium, the brakes carbon-ceramic. The Lambo uses a steel structure, also clothed in carbon.

The cabin of the Lambo is an enveloping cocoon of the hand-made. That's not the wavy stitching, rattly trim and whiff of glue that once characterised Lamborghinis either. It's done with the precision and discipline of the Audi parent, but the flair of the Italians of old. There are, before you ask, no Audi buttons to speak of.

The Corvette feels mass-made, because that's what Corvettes are. This brings huge benefits in ergonomics, including a head-up display, but it makes things feel a mite ordinary, despite the leather-wrapped dash. (Can't complain too much mind: a 911 Turbo's cabin is just a

Boxster's in a Saturday night pulling shirt.) What really does let down the ZR1 is its fast-food seats. They're too flabby and wobbly to hold you against the ZR1's immense forces.

The fact that the ZR1 shares a cabin, a suspension, an electronics system, a transmission and a production line – but not a whole lot else – with the mass-made base Vette is why it's half the price of the Lamborghini. Still £109,000 mind, but half the price. We got this far in the story without mentioning the money because in all honesty, when you're flat on the throttle, squeezing the brakes or going through a full-chat corner, the money doesn't enter into it.

But there is the crux of the issue for people who just don't get the ZR1. It's stuck in a kind of limbo-land. It can deliver the sheer blood-and-guts of a car double its price, so long as your driving style suits this classic knife-edge style. But it looks like a car half its price. And it's just as sensible as the regular Corvette C6.

The Murciélago views the whole notion of sensible with utter disdain. It insists you do things its way, even when that's a bit of a pain in the backside. There are times when my personality simply isn't big enough to cope with that. But given the chance of a proper drive, it would be the one of this pair I'd pick. Not because of its looks or its eff-you personality or its undoubted curiosity value, but because it's such a well-sorted car down the road. ▣

'Apple-pie drifts are there for the taking when the ESP is off, or even when it's in the intermediate "competitive mode"'

INDEX

11

Published in 2010 by BBC Books, an imprint of Ebury Publishing.
a Random House Group Company

Text © TopGear Magazine 2010
Anthology © Woodlands Books 2010

Design and art direction: Charlie Turner

Photographers: Mark Bramley, Lee Brimble, Jonathan Bushell, Jason Furnari,
Barry Hayden, Justin Leighton, James Lipman, John Wycherley
Writers: Jason Barlow, Jeremy Clarkson, Jon Claydon, Pat Devereux, Tom Ford, Richard Hammond,
Paul Horrell, Matt Master, Sam Philip, Ripley & Ripley,
Bill Thomas, Anton Watts, Joe Windsor-Williams

The Random House Group Limited Reg. No. 954009

Addresses for companies within the Random House Group can be found at
www.randomhouse.co.uk

A CIP catalogue record for this book is available from the British Library.

ISBN 978 1 84 990054 6

Penguin Random House is committed to a sustainable future for our business, our readers and our
planet. This book is made from Forest Stewardship Council® certified paper.

Commissioning editor: Lorna Russell
Project editor at BBC Books: Caroline McArthur
Project Editors at TopGear: Bill Thomas and Simon Carrington
Design and art direction: Charlie Turner
Production: Antony Heller

Colour origination by Christopher Rowles
Printed and bound in China by C&C Offset Printing Co., Ltd.

To buy books by your favourite authors and register for offers, visit www.randomhouse.co.uk